Studies in World History

DR. JAMES STOBAUGH

Vol. 3

The Modern Age
to Present
{1900 A.D. to Present}

GOVERNMENT   GEOGRAPHY   ECONOMICS   RELIGION   GOVERNMENT   GEOGRAPHY

RELIGION   HISTORY   GOVERNMENT   GEOGRAPHY   ECONOMICS   RELIGION

TEACHER GUIDE

Includes: Answer Keys

Daily Calendar

Daily Discussion Questions

Weekly Exams

First printing: April 2014

Master Books®, P.O. Box 726, Green Forest, AR 72638

Master Books® is a division of the New Leaf Publishing Group, Inc.

ISBN: 978-0-89051-793-2

Unless otherwise noted, Scripture quotations are from the New King James Version of the Bible.

Printed in the United States of America

Please visit our website for other great titles:
www.masterbooks.net

For information regarding author interviews,
please contact the publicity department at (870) 438-5288

Master Books®
A Division of New Leaf Publishing Group
www.masterbooks.net

Where Creation Inspires Education

Since 1975, Master Books has been providing educational resources based on a biblical worldview to students of all ages. At the heart of these resources is our firm belief in a literal six-day creation, a young earth, the global Flood as revealed in Genesis 1–11, and other vital evidence to help build a critical foundation of scriptural authority for everyone. By equipping students with biblical truths and their key connection to the world of science and history, it is our hope they will be able to defend their faith in a skeptical, fallen world.

If the foundations are destroyed, what can the righteous do?
Psalm 11:3; NKJV

As the largest publisher of creation science materials in the world, Master Books is honored to partner with our authors and educators, including:

Ken Ham of Answers in Genesis

Dr. John Morris and Dr. Jason Lisle of the Institute for Creation Research

Dr. Donald DeYoung and Michael Oard of the Creation Research Society

Dr. James Stobaugh, John Hudson Tiner, Rick and Marilyn Boyer, Dr. Tom DeRosa, Todd Friel, Israel Wayne and so many more!

Whether a preschool learner or a scholar seeking an advanced degree, we offer a wonderful selection of award-winning resources for all ages and educational levels.

But sanctify the Lord God in your hearts, and always be ready
to give a defense to everyone who asks you a reason for the hope
that is in you, with meekness and fear.
1 Peter 3:15; NKJV

Permission to Copy

Lessons for a 34-week course!

Overview: This *Studies in World History Volume 3 Teacher Guide* contains materials for use with *Studies in World History Volume 3*. Materials are organized by book in the following sections:

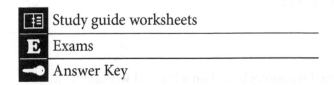

Study guide worksheets	
Exams	
Answer Key	

Features: Each suggested weekly schedule has five easy-to-manage lessons that combine reading, worksheets, and optional exams. Worksheets and exams are perforated and three-hole punched – materials are easy to tear out, hand out, grade, and store. You are encouraged to adjust the schedule and materials needed to best work within your educational program.

Workflow: Students will read the pages in their book and then complete each section of the Teacher Guide. Exams are given at regular intervals with space to record each grade. If used with younger students, they may be given the option of taking open-book exams.

Lesson Scheduling: Space is given for assignment dates. There is flexibility in scheduling. For example, the parent may opt for a M, W, F schedule, rather than a M-F schedule. Each week listed has five days but due to vacations the school work week may not be M–F. Adapt the days to your school schedule. As the student completes each assignment, he/she should put an "X" in the box.

🕐	Approximately 20 to 30 minutes per lesson, five days a week
🔑	Includes answer keys for worksheets and exams
📋	Worksheets for each section
↻	Exams are included to help reinforce learning and provide assessment opportunities
📄	Designed for grades 7 to 9 in a one-year course to earn 1 social studies credit

Dr. James Stobaugh was a Merrill Fellow at Harvard and holds degrees from Vanderbilt and Rutgers universities, and Princeton and Gordon-Conwell seminaries. An experienced teacher, he is a recognized leader in homeschooling and has published numerous books for students and teachers, including a high school history series (American, British, and World), as well as a companion high school literature series. He and his wife Karen have homeschooled their four children since 1985.

Contents

Introduction

The junior high student will see history come to life no matter what his or her pace or ability. Developed by Dr. James Stobaugh, these courses grow in difficulty with each year, preparing students for high school work. This is a comprehensive examination of history, geography, economics, religion, and government systems. This educational set equips students to learn from a starting point of God's creation of the world and move forward with a solid biblically based worldview. Volume 3 focuses on modernism, the world at war, American education, Evangelicalism, modern social problems, and more.

How this course has been developed:

1. Chapters: This course has 34 chapters (representing 34 weeks of study).

2. Lessons: Each chapter has five lessons, taking approximately 20 to 30 minutes each. There is a short reading followed by discussion questions. Some questions require a specific answer from the text, while others are more open ended, leading students to think "outside the box."

3. Weekly exams: This Teacher Guide includes two optional exams for each chapter.

4. Student responsibility: Responsibility to complete this course is on the student. Students are to complete the readings every day, handing their responses in to a parent or teacher for evaluation. This course was designed for students to practice independent learning.

5. Grading: Students turn in assignments to a parent or teacher for grading.

Throughout the student text are the following components:

1. First thoughts: Background on the historical period.

2. Discussion questions: Questions based generally on Bloom's Taxonomy.

3. Concepts: Terms, concepts, and theories to be learned that are bolded for emphasis. Most are listed on the first page of the chapter and in the glossary.

4. History makers: A person(s) who clearly changed the course of history.

5. Historical debate: An examination of historical theories surrounding a period or topic.

First Semester Suggested Daily Schedule

Date	Day	Assignment	Due Date	✓	Grade
		First Semester — First Quarter			

Chapter 1: Modernism: To Rule the Earth

Modernism with its commitment to human ingenuity and to technology was headed toward a huge disaster, but no one in the first part of the 20th century knew that was the case.

Date	Day	Assignment	Due Date	✓	Grade
Week 1	Day 1	Read **Lesson 1 — Modernism** Student Book (SB) Answer Discussion Question Page 21 Lesson Planner (LP)			
	Day 2	Read **Lesson 2 — The Transatlantic Cable** (SB) Answer Discussion Question Page 22 (LP)			
	Day 3	Read **Lesson 3 — Modernism and Literature** (SB) Answer Discussion Question Page 23 (LP)			
	Day 4	Read **Lesson 4 — Modern Art: Tamed by the Middle Class** (SB) Answer Discussion Question Page 24 (LP)			
	Day 5	Read **Lesson 5 — The Sinking of the *Titanic*** (SB) Answer Discussion Question Page 25 (LP) Optional **Lesson 1 Exam** 1 or 2 Page 227–228 (LP)			

Chapter 2: Progressivism: Newsies and Muckrakers

Noble Progressivism was somewhat successful in American society by curving excesses and ameliorating injustices, but ultimately, Progressivism was doomed to fail. It was a political movement that was betrayed by embracing liberal ideology and snobbery.

Date	Day	Assignment	Due Date	✓	Grade
Week 2	Day 6	Read **Lesson 1 — A New Age** (SB) Answer Discussion Question Page 27 (LP)			
	Day 7	Read **Lesson 2 — The Promise of American Life . . .** (SB) Answer Discussion Question Page 28 (LP)			
	Day 8	Read **Lesson 3 — *Newsies*** (SB) Answer Discussion Question Page 29 (LP)			
	Day 9	Read **Lesson 4 — Theodore Roosevelt** (SB) Answer Discussion Question Page 30 (LP)			
	Day 10	Read **Lesson 5 — The Income Tax** (SB) Answer Discussion Question Page 31 (LP) Optional **Lesson 2 Exam** 1 or 2 Page 229–230 (LP)			

Chapter 3: 1900–1914: On the Brink

Resting in the glow of unprecedented prosperity that was so much a part of the late Victorian industrial revolution, the world was naively moving toward an unmitigated disaster that was to be the first of several catastrophic 20th-century wars.

Date	Day	Assignment	Due Date	✓	Grade
Week 3	Day 11	Read **Lesson 1 — The Loss of Faith . . . We Once Believed In** (SB) Answer Discussion Question Page 33 (LP)			
	Day 12	Read **Lesson 2 — The Spirit of the Modern World** (SB) Answer Discussion Question Page 34 (LP)			
	Day 13	Read **Lesson 3 — The German Empire** (SB) Answer Discussion Question Page 35 (LP)			
	Day 14	Read **Lesson 4 — Militarism** (SB) Answer Discussion Question Page 36 (LP)			
	Day 15	Read **Lesson 5 — The Failure of Government** (SB) Answer Discussion Question Page 37 (LP) Optional **Lesson 3 Exam** 1 or 2 Page 231–232 (LP)			

Chapter 4: World at War: World War I Memoirs

This chapter reminds us again that wars are fought by people, not by nations. When all the glory and misery fade, human stories, foibles, and tragedies remain. That is the essence of this chapter, and this is the essence of the future that was to come.

Date	Day	Assignment	Due Date	✓	Grade
Week 4	Day 16	Read **Lesson 1 — An Aviator's Field Book** (SB) Answer Discussion Question Page 39 (LP)			
	Day 17	Read **Lesson 2 — Unknown French Soldier, 1914–1915** (SB) Answer Discussion Question Page 40 (LP)			
	Day 18	Read **Lesson 3 — Anonymous, *Diary of a Nursing Sister . . .*** (SB) Answer Discussion Question Page 41 (LP)			
	Day 19	Read **Lesson 4 — Letters of Lt.-Col. George Brenton Laurie** (SB) Answer Discussion Question Page 42 (LP)			
	Day 20	Read **Lesson 5 — *The Greater Love*** (SB) Answer Discussion Question Page 43 (LP) Optional **Lesson 4 Exam** 1 or 2 Page 233–234 (LP)			

Chapter 5: Modern America: The Cultural Revolution

Perhaps the merry-go-round is the best metaphor for what was becoming Modern America. Up and down, around and around, the passenger was blessed with a cornucopia of marvelous experiences. But the problem was, when the ride was over, the fortunate passenger was at the same place he began.

Date	Day	Assignment	Due Date	✓	Grade
Week 5	Day 21	Read **Lesson 1 — Mass Communication** (SB) Answer Discussion Question Page 45 (LP)			
	Day 22	Read **Lesson 2 — The Theme Park** (SB) Answer Discussion Question Page 46 (LP)			
	Day 23	Read **Lesson 3 — National Anxiety** (SB) Answer Discussion Question Page 47 (LP)			
	Day 24	Read **Lesson 4 — The University** (SB) Answer Discussion Question Page 48 (LP)			
	Day 25	Read **Lesson 5 — Harvard or Heaven: The Decline . . .** (SB) Answer Discussion Question Page 49 (LP) Optional **Lesson 5 Exam** 1 or 2 Page 235–236 (LP)			

Chapter 6: The Russian Revolution: Fighting with No Ethics

The French Revolution started with the most laudable of purposes but morphed into an unmitigated disaster within one generation. The Russian Revolution, however, from the beginning had an insatiable appetite for blood and consumed its people.

Date	Day	Assignment	Due Date	✓	Grade
Week 6	Day 26	Read **Lesson 1 — Russian History, 1905–1917** (SB) Answer Discussion Question Page 51 (LP)			
	Day 27	Read **Lesson 2 — Summary** (SB) Answer Discussion Question Page 52 (LP)			
	Day 28	Read **Lesson 3 — Communism Vs. Democracy** (SB) Answer Discussion Question Page 53 (LP)			
	Day 29	Read **Lesson 4 — Ten Days that Shook the World . . .** (SB) Answer Discussion Question Page 54 (LP)			
	Day 30	Read **Lesson 5 — "How Should a Christian View . . .** (SB) Answer Discussion Question Page 55 (LP) Optional **Lesson 6 Exam** 1 or 2 Page 237–238 (LP)			

Chapter 7: The Volstead Act: Legislating Morality

Prohibition was a noble and highly effective experiment but soundly rejected by almost all social critics. Too bad. The Volstead Act accomplished all that it intended but proved conclusively to American politicians that legislating morality should never be tried again.

	Day	Assignment			
Week 7	Day 31	Read **Lesson 1 — Prohibition** (SB) Answer Discussion Question Page 57 (LP)			
	Day 32	Read **Lesson 2 — Women's Christian Temperance Union** (SB) Answer Discussion Question Page 58 (LP)			
	Day 33	Read **Lesson 3 — Speech to the Women's Christian . . .** (SB) Answer Discussion Question Page 59 (LP)			
	Day 34	Read **Lesson 4 — The Mafia** (SB) Answer Discussion Question Page 60 (LP)			
	Day 35	Read **Lesson 5 — Al Capone** (SB) Answer Discussion Question Page 61 (LP) Optional **Lesson 7 Exam** 1 or 2 Page 239–240 (LP)			

Chapter 8: American Education: A Dream Deferred

Public education was doomed from the start for the simple reason that it was an oxymoron—education is never public—it is the most private of human endeavors and will always be accomplished best by the parents God has placed in authority over children.

	Day	Assignment			
Week 8	Day 36	Read **Lesson 1 — Public Education** (SB) Answer Discussion Question Page 63 (LP)			
	Day 37	Read **Lesson 2 — Primary Source, 1831** (SB) Answer Discussion Question Page 64 (LP)			
	Day 38	Read **Lesson 3 — Horace Mann** (SB) Answer Discussion Question Page 65 (LP)			
	Day 39	Read **Lesson 4 — Secondary Essay** (SB) Answer Discussion Question Page 66 (LP)			
	Day 40	Read **Lesson 5 — Homeschooling: Back to the Future?** (SB) Answer Discussion Question Page 67 (LP) Optional **Lesson 8 Exam** 1 or 2 Page 241–242 (LP)			

Chapter 9: Evangelicalism: Salvation and Biblical Authority

From the beginning, America was an evangelical Christian nation—it built its universities to train a Christian leadership cadre, for it earnestly sought to be governed by, to have its culture created by, evangelical Christians. Now the retreat grows more rapid.

	Day	Assignment			
Week 9	Day 41	Read **Lesson 1 — Early Evangelicalism** (SB) Answer Discussion Question Page 69 (LP)			
	Day 42	Read **Lesson 2 — 18th- and 19th-Century Evangelicalism** (SB) Answer Discussion Question Page 70 (LP)			
	Day 43	Read **Lesson 3 — 20th Century** (SB) Answer Discussion Question Page 71 (LP)			
	Day 44	Read **Lesson 4 — The Scandal of the Evangelical Mind, . . .** (SB) Answer Discussion Question Page 72 (LP)			
	Day 45	Read **Lesson 5 — The Author's Theological Statement** (SB) Answer Discussion Question Page 73 (LP) Optional **Lesson 9 Exam** 1 or 2 Page 243–244 (LP)			

First Semester — Second Quarter

Chapter 10: The Scopes Trial: The Fool, Fixed on His Folly

The Scopes Trail was the rehearsal of a modern tragedy that would be played out from now on in American history. America entered a sort of Dark Age at the termination of the Scopes Trial on that scorching summer afternoon in late July 1925.

Week 1	Day 46	Read **Lesson 1 — Early Evangelicalism** (SB) Answer Discussion Question Page 75 (LP)			
	Day 47	Read **Lesson 2 — The Scopes Trial** (SB) Answer Discussion Question Page 76 (LP)			
	Day 48	Read **Lesson 3 — The Necessity for Believing in Six . . .** (SB) Answer Discussion Question Page 77 (LP)			
	Day 49	Read **Lesson 4 — William Jennings Bryan** (SB) Answer Discussion Question Page 78 (LP)			
	Day 50	Read **Lesson 5 — A Cultural Revolution** (SB) Answer Discussion Question Page 79 (LP) Optional **Lesson 10 Exam** 1 or 2 Page 245–246 (LP)			

Chapter 11: Germany 1871–1945: A Failed Democracy

Stillborn, though, shackled with unjust reparations and the catastrophic Great Depression, the Weimar Republic became a symbol of unprecedented hedonism and a launching pad for the most profound evil mankind was to know in the 20th century.

Week 2	Day 51	Read **Lesson 1 — Weimar Republic** (SB) Answer Discussion Question Page 81 (LP)			
	Day 52	Read **Lesson 2 — The Weimar Economy** (SB) Answer Discussion Question Page 82 (LP)			
	Day 53	Read **Lesson 3 — Impact of Inflation** (SB) Answer Discussion Question Page 83 (LP)			
	Day 54	Read **Lesson 4 — Sociology: The Cabaret** (SB) Answer Discussion Question Page 84 (LP)			
	Day 55	Read **Lesson 5 — What We Can Learn from 1920s Germany** (SB) Answer Discussion Question Page 85 (LP) Optional **Lesson 11 Exam** 1 or 2 Page 247–248 (LP)			

Chapter 12: The New Deal: Failure of the Liberal State

The New Deal was a shrill cry of defeat as a people and a nation floundered in an unprecedented economic depression. Unfortunately this apogee of human effort spawned unanticipated results that would turn tragic.

Week 3	Day 56	Read **Lesson 1 — The Great Depression and New Deal** (SB) Answer Discussion Question Page 87 (LP)			
	Day 57	Read **Lesson 2 — Franklin Delano Roosevelt's First Inaugural Address, March 4, 1933** (SB) Answer Discussion Question Page 88 (LP)			
	Day 58	Read **Lesson 3 — Social Legislation** (SB) Answer Discussion Question Page 89 (LP)			
	Day 59	Read **Lesson 4 — The Failure of the Positive Liberal State** (SB) Answer Discussion Question Page 90 (LP)			
	Day 60	Read **Lesson 5 — Political Cartoons — Herb Block** (SB) Answer Discussion Question Page 91 (LP) Optional **Lesson 12 Exam** 1 or 2 Page 249–250 (LP)			

Chapter 13: Born in Slavery: Slave Narratives 1936–1938

The WPA Slave Narratives project was perhaps the only good result of the New Deal. These insightful, delightful narratives provide all Americans, for all time, with a priceless oral history of a most lamentable time of American history.

Date	Day	Assignment	Due Date	✓	Grade
Week 4	Day 61	Read **Lesson 1 — Mary Reynolds, Dallas, Texas** (SB) Answer Discussion Question Page 93 (LP)			—
	Day 62	Read **Lesson 2 — Emma Crockett, Livingston, Alabama** (SB) Answer Discussion Question Page 94 (LP)			
	Day 63	Read **Lesson 3 — Walter Calloway, Birmingham, Alabama** (SB) Answer Discussion Question Page 95 (LP)			
	Day 64	Read **Lesson 4 — Richard Toler, Cincinnati, Ohio** (SB) Answer Discussion Question Page 96 (LP)			
	Day 65	Read **Lesson 5 — Ben Horry, Murrells Inlet, South Carolina** (SB) Answer Discussion Question Page 97 (LP) Optional **Lesson 13 Exam** 1 or 2 Page 251–252 (LP)			

Chapter 14: World War II: Primary Sources

The fears, wants, and dreams of these Americans are, after all, the real story of World War II. We hear in their whispers, their cries, their outrage, their frustration, their simple desires. This is real history!

Date	Day	Assignment	Due Date	✓	Grade
Week 5	Day 66	Read **Lesson 1 — Leona Cox, Red Cross Nurse** (SB) Answer Discussion Question Page 99 (LP)			
	Day 67	Read **Lesson 2 — Andrew Melendrez Sr., Sergeant, . . .** (SB) Answer Discussion Question Page 100 (LP)			
	Day 68	Read **Lesson 3 — John William Manix, U. S. Army, . . .** (SB) Answer Discussion Question Page 101 (LP)			
	Day 69	Read **Lesson 4 — Carlisle Evans, U. S. Marine Corps, . . .** (SB) Answer Discussion Question Page 102 (LP)			
	Day 70	Read **Lesson 5 — Robert M. Alexander, U.S. Army . . .** (SB) Answer Discussion Question Page 103 (LP) Optional **Lesson 14 Exam** 1 or 2 Page 253–254 (LP)			

Chapter 15: Genocide: Intention to Destroy

The Holocaust remains both the shocking monument to Modernism and a warning to future generations who would seek to divorce their knowledge from their faith. It took the best of 20th century technology and ingenuity to create the most heinous crime of the 20th century.

Date	Day	Assignment	Due Date	✓	Grade
Week 6	Day 71	Read **Lesson 1 — Overview** (SB) Answer Discussion Question Page 105 (LP)			
	Day 72	Read **Lesson 2 — German Definition of a Jew** (SB) Answer Discussion Question Page 106 (LP)			
	Day 73	Read **Lesson 3 — Ghettoization and Resettlement** (SB) Answer Discussion Question Page 107 (LP)			
	Day 74	Read **Lesson 4 — Killing Centers** (SB) Answer Discussion Question Page 108 (LP)			
	Day 75	Read **Lesson 5 — A Devout Meditation . . . Adolf Eichmann** (SB) Answer Discussion Question Page 109 (LP) Optional **Lesson 15 Exam** 1 or 2 Page 255–256 (LP)			

Chapter 16: The Cold War: Geopolitical Conflict

The Cold War created frustration and fear—endlessly! It was fought in space, in former colonies, and on the plains of Europe. The United States won by default—the Soviet Union could not sustain the cost of continuing a war that was not really a war.

Week 7	Day 76	Read **Lesson 1 — The Origins of the Cold War** (SB) Answer Discussion Question Page 111 (LP)			
	Day 77	Read **Lesson 2 — A Geopolitical Conflict** (SB) Answer Discussion Question Page 112 (LP)			
	Day 78	Read **Lesson 3 — Korean War: A Limited War** (SB) Answer Discussion Question Page 113 (LP)			
	Day 79	Read **Lesson 4 — The Cuban Missile Crisis: At the Brink** (SB) Answer Discussion Question Page 114 (LP)			
	Day 80	Read **Lesson 5 — Vietnam War** (SB) Answer Discussion Question Page 115 (LP) Optional **Lesson 16 Exam** 1 or 2 Page 257–258 (LP)			

Chapter 17: The Cinema: A Cultural Force in Society

Movies, like television, have become the epistemological center of the universe. The problem with movies is that they are not real, can never be real. But they define our heroes and heroes, our fashions, our morality.

Week 8	Day 81	Read **Lesson 1 — Hollywood as History** (SB) Answer Discussion Question Page 117 (LP)			
	Day 82	Read **Lesson 2 — The Pre-History of Motion Pictures** (SB) Answer Discussion Question Page 118 (LP)			
	Day 83	Read **Lesson 3 — The Movies as a Cultural Battleground** (SB) Answer Discussion Question Page 119 (LP)			
	Day 84	Read **Lesson 4 — The Searchers — A Movie Review** (SB) Answer Discussion Question Page 120 (LP)			
	Day 85	Read **Lesson 5 — The Future of Cinema?** (SB) Answer Discussion Question Page 121 (LP) Optional **Lesson 17 Exam** 1 or 2 Page 259–260 (LP)			

Chapter 18: Rock 'n' Roll: Times Were A-Changin'

From the heart of jazz emerged the most iconoclastic cultural movement in world history: Rock 'n' Roll. It was music; it was theology. It was the anthem of a culture war that is still being waged across this land.

Week 9	Day 86	Read **Lesson 1 — Origins** (SB) Answer Discussion Question Page 123 (LP)			
	Day 87	Read **Lesson 2 — A Music Revolution** (SB) Answer Discussion Question Page 124 (LP)			
	Day 88	Read **Lesson 3 — The Times They Were A-Changin'** (SB) Answer Discussion Question Page 125 (LP)			
	Day 89	Read **Lesson 4 — Religion and Rock 'n' Roll** (SB) Answer Discussion Question Page 126 (LP)			
	Day 90	Read **Lesson 5 — "40 Years Later, Woodstock's Impact . . . "** (SB) Answer Discussion Question Page 127 (LP) Optional **Lesson 18 Exam** 1 or 2 Page 261–262 (LP)			
		Midterm Grade			

Second Semester Suggested Daily Schedule

Date	Day	Assignment	Due Date	✓	Grade
		Second Semester — Third Quarter			

Chapter 19: The 20th Century: Radical Revolutions

A century might have one or two revolutions, but the 20th century saw five or six. The technological revolution, the computer revolution, the drug revolution—these are only a few.

Date	Day	Assignment	Due Date	✓	Grade
Week 1	Day 91	Read **Lesson 1 — A Century of Change** (SB) Answer Discussion Question Page 129 (LP)			
	Day 92	Read **Lesson 2 — 20th-Century Revolutions** (SB) Answer Discussion Question Page 130 (LP)			
	Day 93	Read **Lesson 3 — A Youth Revolution** (SB) Answer Discussion Question Page 131 (LP)			
	Day 94	Read **Lesson 4 — Prosperity** (SB) Answer Discussion Question Page 132 (LP)			
	Day 95	Read **Lesson 5 — Free at Last** (SB) Answer Discussion Question Page 133 (LP) Optional **Lesson 19 Exam** 1 or 2 Page 263–264 (LP)			

Chapter 20: 1960s: The Death of Outrage

No longer content to be images of the generation ahead of them, young people wanted change. The changes affected education, values, lifestyles, laws, and entertainment. The teenagers of the 1960s are the ancient mariners of the 21st century.

Date	Day	Assignment	Due Date	✓	Grade
Week 2	Day 96	Read **Lesson 1 — Shadows in Paradise** (SB) Answer Discussion Question Page 135 (LP)			
	Day 97	Read **Lesson 2 — Ralph Nader . . . Consumer Movement** (SB) Answer Discussion Question Page 136 (LP)			
	Day 98	Read **Lesson 3 — The City: Broken Promises** (SB) Answer Discussion Question Page 137 (LP)			
	Day 99	Read **Lesson 4 — A Book Review** (SB) Answer Discussion Question Page 138 (LP)			
	Day 100	Read **Lesson 5 — The Death of the Heroes** (SB) Answer Discussion Question Page 139 (LP) Optional **Lesson 20 Exam** 1 or 2 Page 265–266 (LP)			

Chapter 21: American Government: A Balance of Power

The US government is a beautiful thing. It not perfect, but it is the best that man can make. Inherently suspicious of strong individuals, but aware of the dangers that uncontrolled movements of people can bring, the government of the United States invites the best it can from its people.

Date	Day	Assignment	Due Date	✓	Grade
Week 3	Day 101	Read **Lesson 1 — General Government** (SB) Answer Discussion Question Page 141 (LP)			
	Day 102	Read **Lesson 2 — Terms — Forms of Government** (SB) Answer Discussion Question Page 142 (LP)			
	Day 103	Read **Lesson 3 — Executive Branch** (SB) Answer Discussion Question Page 143 (LP)			
	Day 104	Read **Lesson 4 — The Legislative Branch** (SB) Answer Discussion Question Page 144 (LP)			
	Day 105	Read **Lesson 5 — The Judiciary** (SB) Answer Discussion Question Page 145 (LP) Optional **Lesson 21 Exam** 1 or 2 Page 267–268 (LP)			

Chapter 22: Space Program: One Giant Leap for Mankind

The race to the moon, the race into space, is the stuff of dreams. It was one of the only imaginings that was promised by Buck Rogers and other comic book heroes that really happened. Indeed the history of space exporation was spectacular!

	Day	Assignment			
Week 4	Day 106	Read **Lesson 1 — Overview of Space Travel** (SB) Answer Discussion Question Page 147 (LP)			
	Day 107	Read **Lesson 2 — Wernher von Braun** (SB) Answer Discussion Question Page 148 (LP)			
	Day 108	Read **Lesson 3 — Space Disasters** (SB) Answer Discussion Question Page 149 (LP)			
	Day 109	Read **Lesson 4 — The Future of Space Travel** (SB) Answer Discussion Question Page 150 (LP)			
	Day 110	Read **Lesson 5 — UFOs** (SB) Answer Discussion Question Page 151 (LP) Optional **Lesson 22 Exam** 1 or 2 Page 269–270 (LP)			

Chapter 23: Profound Changes: The Modern Family

Societies are so tightly woven that changes in one domain radiated through others and eventually altered how people think and feel. The result was a shift from tradition to "modernity" and a rejection of almost everything sacred.

	Day	Assignment			
Week 5	Day 111	Read **Lesson 1 — The Modern Family** (SB) Answer Discussion Question Page 153 (LP)			
	Day 112	Read **Lesson 2 — Fatherless America: Confronting Our . . .** (SB) Answer Discussion Question Page 154 (LP)			
	Day 113	Read **Lesson 3 — Feminism** (SB) Answer Discussion Question Page 155 (LP)			
	Day 114	Read **Lesson 4 — A Study of Galatians 3:28, . . .** (SB) Answer Discussion Question Page 156 (LP)			
	Day 115	Read **Lesson 5 — A Modern Family in Literature** (SB) Answer Discussion Question Page 157 (LP) Optional **Lesson 23 Exam** 1 or 2 Page 271–272 (LP)			

Chapter 24: A City Church: The City of God

In the 1890s, the outer border of settlement was six miles away. By annexing surrounding lands and filling in bays, cities grew larger, allowing for greater differentiation in the use of space. The city church responded with varying degrees of success.

	Day	Assignment			
Week 6	Day 116	Read **Lesson 1 — "Our City: God's Creation"** (SB) Answer Discussion Question Page 159 (LP)			
	Day 117	Read **Lesson 2 — Problems of Urbanization** (SB) Answer Discussion Question Page 160 (LP)			
	Day 118	Read **Lesson 3 — The Urban Church, Part I** (SB) Answer Discussion Question Page 161 (LP)			
	Day 119	Read **Lesson 4 — The Urban Church, Part II** (SB) Answer Discussion Question Page 162 (LP)			
	Day 120	Read **Lesson 5 — From Antioch to Vancouver** (SB) Answer Discussion Question Page 163 (LP) Optional **Lesson 24 Exam** 1 or 2 Page 273–274 (LP)			

Chapter 25: Post-Modernism: Miserable but Enjoying It

The term "Post-Modernism" comes from its critique of the "Modernist" scientific mentality of objectivity and progress associated with the Enlightenment. Post-Modernism offers both a challenge and an opportunity to the Christian community.

Week 7	Day 121	Read **Lesson 1 — Definition and Origin** (SB) Answer Discussion Question Page 165 (LP)			
	Day 122	Read **Lesson 2 — Post-Modern Architecture** (SB) Answer Discussion Question Page 166 (LP)			
	Day 123	Read **Lesson 3 — Post-Modern Justice** (SB) Answer Discussion Question Page 167 (LP)			
	Day 124	Read **Lesson 4 — Christian Voices** (SB) Answer Discussion Question Page 168 (LP)			
	Day 125	Read **Lesson 5 — Ministry to the Post-Modern Generation** (SB) Answer Discussion Question Page 169 (LP) Optional **Lesson 25 Exam** 1 or 2 Page 275–276 (LP)			

Chapter 26: Politics and More: The State of America

Some of the most important cultural transformations are the result of countless individuals in their daily lives: the emergence of the modern family; the rise of the modern concept of privacy; the growth of individualism.

Week 8	Day 126	Read **Lesson 1 — Food in America** (SB) Answer Discussion Question Page 171 (LP)			
	Day 127	Read **Lesson 2 — Obvious but False: Common Views of . . .** (SB) Answer Discussion Question Page 172 (LP)			
	Day 128	Read **Lesson 3 — The Tea Party Movement** (SB) Answer Discussion Question Page 173 (LP)			
	Day 129	Read **Lesson 4 — The Recession of 2008** (SB) Answer Discussion Question Page 174 (LP)			
	Day 130	Read **Lesson 5 — The Future of America: Elisha's Tears, . . .** (SB) Answer Discussion Question Page 175 (LP) Optional **Lesson 26 Exam** 1 or 2 Page 277–278 (LP)			

Chapter 27: 20th-Century Saints: Culture Warriors

Evangelicals have not always put their best foot forward, only grudgingly willing to grapple with complexity and doubt. Evangelicals' world is a one of absolutes. At the same time, the short biographies of these four saints put a human face on the issue.

Week 9	Day 131	Read **Lesson 1 — Oswald Chambers (1874–1917)** (SB) Answer Discussion Question Page 177 (LP)			
	Day 132	Read **Lesson 2 — C.S. Lewis (1898–1963), . . .** (SB) Answer Discussion Question Page 178 (LP)			
	Day 133	Read **Lesson 3 — Thomas Merton (1915–1968)** (SB) Answer Discussion Question Page 179 (LP)			
	Day 134	Read **Lesson 4 — Francis Schaeffer (1912–1984)** (SB) Answer Discussion Question Page 180 (LP)			
	Day 135	Read **Lesson 5 — Mother Teresa (1910–1997), . . .** (SB) Answer Discussion Question Page 181 (LP) Optional **Lesson 27 Exam** 1 or 2 Page 279–280 (LP)			

Date	Day	Assignment	Due Date	✓	Grade

Chapter 28: The University: Belshazzar's Feast

God's favor is on the evangelical community. Never have we had a greater opportunity to attend the best schools in the country. What are we to do? The university was lost to the Christian in fights over Darwinism and higher criticism of the Bible.

	Day	Assignment			
Week 1	Day 136	Read **Lesson 1 — The Origin of the University** (SB) Answer Discussion Question Page 183 (LP)			
	Day 137	Read **Lesson 2 — Prospering in the Secular University** (SB) Answer Discussion Question Page 184 (LP)			
	Day 138	Read **Lesson 3 — Harvard and Heaven — . . .** (SB) Answer Discussion Question Page 185 (LP)			
	Day 139	Read **Lesson 4 — A Book Review** (SB) Answer Discussion Question Page 186 (LP)			
	Day 140	Read **Lesson 5 — Harvard University Charter** (SB) Answer Discussion Question Page 187 (LP) Optional **Lesson 28 Exam** 1 or 2 Page 281–282 (LP)			

Chapter 29: Shadow History: Second-Page Stories

After examining the American love affair with oil consumption, we examine the future potential of fuel consumption. Finally, we examine the perennial and pervasive violence that plagues America.

	Day	Assignment			
Week 2	Day 141	Read **Lesson 1 — Hostages** (SB) Answer Discussion Question Page 189 (LP)			
	Day 142	Read **Lesson 2 — The Politics of Oil** (SB) Answer Discussion Question Page 190 (LP)			
	Day 143	Read **Lesson 3 — Energy Future, Report of the Energy . . .** (SB) Answer Discussion Question Page 191 (LP)			
	Day 144	Read **Lesson 4 — Assassination** (SB) Answer Discussion Question Page 192 (LP)			
	Day 145	Read **Lesson 5 — Pervading Hopelessness** (SB) Answer Discussion Question Page 193 (LP) Optional **Lesson 29 Exam** 1 or 2 Page 283–284 (LP)			

Chapter 30: United Europe: Foundational Changes Across the Sea

A united Europe would have been an oxymoron fifty years ago, but today it is a reality. Will it last? What impact will this unified Europe have on the United States?

	Day	Assignment			
Week 3	Day 146	Read **Lesson 1 — United States of Europe** (SB) Answer Discussion Question Page 195 (LP)			
	Day 147	Read **Lesson 2 — The EU** (SB) Answer Discussion Question Page 196 (LP)			
	Day 148	Read **Lesson 3 — Free Trade** (SB) Answer Discussion Question Page 197 (LP)			
	Day 149	Read **Lesson 4 — America vs EU** (SB) Answer Discussion Question Page 198 (LP)			
	Day 150	Read **Lesson 5 — "Worlds Apart on the Vision Thing"** (SB) Answer Discussion Question Page 199 (LP) Optional **Lesson 30 Exam** 1 or 2 Page 285–286 (LP)			

Chapter 31: A Transforming Revolution: The Chinese Century

Some are sceptical of the view that China's huge internal stresses—from dysfunctional banks to religious unrest—have pushed it to the verge of catastrophe. And others have some reservations. One wonders if China can or will. We will see.

	Day	Assignment			
	Day 151	Read **Lesson 1 — And There Was China** (SB) Answer Discussion Question Page 201 (LP)			
	Day 152	Read **Lesson 2 — Republican China (1911–1949)** (SB) Answer Discussion Question Page 202 (LP)			
Week 4	Day 153	Read **Lesson 3 — The People's Republic of China (1949–)** (SB) Answer Discussion Question Page 203 (LP)			
	Day 154	Read **Lesson 4 — Christians in China: Is the Country . . .** (SB) Answer Discussion Question Page 204 (LP)			
	Day 155	Read **Lesson 5 — The Chinese Century** (SB) Answer Discussion Question Page 205 (LP) Optional **Lesson 31 Exam** 1 or 2 Page 287–288 (LP)			

Chapter 32: Terrorism: Tactics and Strategies

The phrase "War on Terror" was first used by US President George W. Bush to denote a global military, political, and ideological struggle against organizations designated as terrorist and regimes that were accused of having a connection to them.

	Day	Assignment			
	Day 156	Read **Lesson 1 — Terrorism** (SB) Answer Discussion Question Page 207 (LP)			
	Day 157	Read **Lesson 2 — Terrorism, A.D. 100 to 1400** (SB) Answer Discussion Question Page 208 (LP)			
Week 5	Day 158	Read **Lesson 3 — Terrorism in the 20th and 21st Centuries** (SB) Answer Discussion Question Page 209 (LP)			
	Day 159	Read **Lesson 4 — Case Study: Sons of Liberty: Patriots or . . .** (SB) Answer Discussion Question Page 210 (LP)			
	Day 160	Read **Lesson 5 — White House: War on Terrorism Is Over** (SB) Answer Discussion Question Page 211 (LP) Optional **Lesson 32 Exam** 1 or 2 Page 289–290 (LP)			

Chapter 33: Apocalypse: End of All Things

In the 1950s and 1960s many people were predicting that the world would end in the next twenty years, destroyed by a nuclear holocaust. It all seemed so surreal.

	Day	Assignment			
	Day 161	Read **Lesson 1 — Pandemic** (SB) Answer Discussion Question Page 213 (LP)			
	Day 162	Read **Lesson 2 — Global Warming or Not — Two Views** (SB) Answer Discussion Question Page 214 (LP)			
Week 6	Day 163	Read **Lesson 3** — Nuclear War (SB) Answer Discussion Question Page 215 (LP)			
	Day 164	Read **Lesson 4 — Overpopulation** (SB) Answer Discussion Question Page 216 (LP)			
	Day 165	Read **Lesson 5 — Competing Views of Eschatology** (SB) Answer Discussion Question Page 217 (LP) Optional **Lesson 33 Exam** 1 or 2 Page 291–292 (LP)			

Chapter 34: Futurology: How Should We Then Live?

Futurology is a predictive science that only recently has gained credibility. What does the near future hold? The distant future? What will American society look like in 2030? We will look at several people who try and look into the next few years and predict what dreams may come.

	Day	Assignment			
Week 7	Day 166	Read **Lesson 1 — Futurology** (SB) Answer Discussion Question Page 219 (LP)			
	Day 167	Read **Lesson 2 — War of the Worlds, Orson Welles, and . . .** (SB) Answer Discussion Question Page 220 (LP)			
	Day 168	Read **Lesson 3 — 1984** (SB) Answer Discussion Question Page 221 (LP)			
	Day 169	Read **Lesson 4 — Brave New World** (SB) Answer Discussion Question Page 222 (LP)			
	Day 170	Read **Lesson 5 — A Short Story — "By the Waters of . . ."** (SB) Answer Discussion Question Page 223 (LP) Optional **Lesson 34 Exam** 1 or 2 Page 293–294 (LP)			
		Semester Grade			

Daily Worksheets

Discussion Questions:

Art historian Clement Greenberg states, "The essence of Modernism lies, as I see it, in the use of characteristic methods of a discipline to criticize the discipline itself, not in order to subvert it but in order to entrench it more firmly in its area of competence. The philosopher Immanuel Kant used logic to establish the limits of logic, and while he withdrew much from its old jurisdiction, logic was left all the more secure in what there remained to it." Modernism, in its attempt to attack everything traditional, created an autocratic liberalism. Explain.

Discussion Questions:

Why did a transatlantic cable have such importance to Modernists?

Discussion Questions:

Which passage has Modernist tendencies and why?

How do I love thee? Let me count the ways.
I love thee to the depth and breadth and height
My soul can reach, when feeling out of sight
For the ends of my Being and ideal Grace.
I love thee to the level of everyday's
Most quiet need, by sun and candlelight.
I love thee freely, as men strive for Right;
I love thee purely, as they turn from Praise.
I love thee with the passion put to use
In my old griefs, and with my childhood's faith.
I love thee with a love I seemed to lose
With my lost saints—I love thee with the breath,
Smiles, tears, of all my life! And, if God choose,
I shall but love thee better after death.
—Elizabeth Barrett Browning .

That is the worst moment, when you feel you have lost
The desires for all that was most desirable,
Before you are contented with what you can desire;
Before you know what is left to be desired;
And you go on wishing that you could desire
What desire has left behind. But you cannot understand.
How could you understand what it is to feel old?
—From T. S. Eliot, "The Cocktail Party" (1949)

Discussion Questions:

The underlying assumptions at work in modern art represent, in microcosm, the problem of Modernism in general. Modern art insists that the artist, by virtue of special dispensation, should express the finer things of humanity through a purely abstract, and entirely personal, understanding and mode of expression. This purely visual art made it an autonomous sphere of activity, completely separate from the everyday world of social and political life. Also, it is separate from history and the lessons learned from history. The self-determining nature of visual art meant that questions asked of it could be properly put, and answered, only in its own terms. Modernism's "history" was constructed through reference only to itself. Why does this spell trouble for Modernism?

Discussion Questions:

The sinking of the *Titanic* was a severe blow to Modernism. The engineering feat of the 20th century, the unsinkable *Titanic* was the poster boy of Modernism. It combined the latest technological advances of the age and the exorbitant luxuries of the same age. On the *Titanic* one traveled in luxury and in technology unrivaled in human history. Yet, ironically, in a little over two hours it sank with the loss of thousands of lives. What lessons can we learn from such a tragedy?

Discussion Questions:

A majority of Americans, who were very active in their pro-life, anti-abortion Protestant and Roman Catholic Church, opposed Sanger's intervention in the private affairs of citizens. But the government did this anyway. Why?

Discussion Questions:

Summarize Herbert Croly's views from today's reading.

Discussion Questions:

Watch the *Newsies* movie and compare it to what actually happened in the 1899 labor strike.

Discussion Questions:

How did Roosevelt expand the power of the presidency, and why was such a president wildly popular in the Progressive era?

Discussion Questions:

Predict what problems would result from an income tax over the next few decades.

Discussion Questions:

Why was it so ironic that World War I occurred at all?

Discussion Questions:

A critic argues, "Ours is a society which no longer firmly believes in anything as certain; it is a society which has lost its confidence in itself as the most advanced civilization in the world. Ours is the age of uncertainty in which all theories and sets of values hold a kernel of truth, but none of them is absolute. The emancipation that Eksteins focuses on is not solely the result of the German spirit that demanded emancipation, but rather the result of our society losing confidence in itself and being forced to accept new (or old) ideas , lifestyles and values as being equally valid with those of the Enlightenment, which constituted the bedrock of society throughout the 19th century. Our obsession with death, movement (or change) and newness can as well be seen as a result of the modern man's uncertainty and desire to find some answers in an unclear world. Myths are more important than ever because they compensate for the mystique and meaning which has been drained out of the modern people's lives, who longer know what to believe in." What are myths, and what myths motivate us today?

Discussion Questions:

Why was Germany, arguably, the primary cause of World War I?

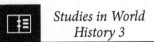
Discussion Questions:

Why was World War I unlike any other previous European War?

Discussion Questions:

Why were European governments so ineffectual in 1914?

Discussion Questions:

Oswald Bölcke was never found. He was missing in action. Can you imagine how his family felt? Research your own community, and find out if there are MIAs (missing in action) in the Vietnam War or more recent wars. If there are, research who one of these men were.

Discussion Questions:

Clutton-Brock, a comrade in arms, writes: "These letters reveal to us a new type of soldier, a new type of hero, almost a new type of man; one who can be brave without any animal consolations, who can endure without any romantic illusions, and, what is more, one who can have faith without any formal revelation. For there is nothing in the letters more interesting than the religion constantly expressed or implied in them.

"He seems afraid to give any artistic expression to his own faith, lest he should falsify it by over-expression, lest it should seem to be more accomplished than it is. He will not even try to take delight in it; he is almost fanatically an intellectual ascetic; and yet again and again he affirms a faith, which he will hardly consent to specify by uttering the name of God. He is shy about it, as if it might be refuted if it were expressed in any dogmatic terms. So many victories seem to have been won over faith in the modern world that his will not throw down any challenge. If it is to live, it must escape the notice of the vulgar triumphing skeptics, and even of the doubting habits of his own mind. Yet it does live its own humble and hesitating life; and in its hesitations and its humility is its strength. Any eager bishop as a lost sheep returning repentant to the fold could not acclaim him; but he is not lost, nor is the universe to him anything but a home and the dear city of God even in the trenches." Do you agree with Brock's assessment of his comrade? Why or why not?

Discussion Questions:

Pretend that you are this nurse's pastor. What would you say to comfort her?

Discussion Questions:

It was highly irregular for an officer of a rank higher than a captain to lead a charge, yet, on March 11, Lt. Colonel Laurie chose to do this. Why?

Discussion Questions:

One of the high points of this memoir was the moment when this Roman Catholic chaplain is invited to dine with Salvation Army workers, and indeed, the priest is asked to say grace! In peacetime England, the Protestant Salvation Army and the Roman Catholic Church were tacit enemies. Yet, in the front lines, they were great friends. Why?

Discussion Questions:

Why was objectivity an early casualty of mass communication?

Discussion Questions:

Amusement parks, in the short run, offered an alternative to beer halls and bars. Predict what sort of problems might arise in the future.

Discussion Questions:

Future Shock is a book written by the futurist Alvin Toffler in 1970. In the book, Toffler defines the term "future shock" as "too much change in too short a period of time." All this change causes stress and disorientation. Was Toffler right? If so, can you give an example?

Discussion Questions:

How did the American university change in the early part of the 20th century?

Discussion Questions:

Do you feel that God may be calling you to a secular university? Why or why not? If so, what can you do to prepare?

Discussion Questions:

Is there anything at this point in 1905 that Czar Nicholas could have done to stop the later 1917 Russian Revolution from occurring?

Discussion Questions:

What caused the 1917 Russian Revolution?

Discussion Questions:

Compare and contrast Communism and Democracy.

Discussion Questions:

John Reed was an American journalist who experienced first hand the Bolshevik Revolution. Where do his sympathies lie?

Discussion Questions:

Summarize Martin Luther King Jr.'s views of Communism from today's lesson.

Discussion Questions:

Many Americans compare present legislation about marijuana to the Volstead Act. Just as the Volstead Act could not be enforced, they claim that laws about marijuana are unenforceable, thus they should be repealed. Do you agree?

Discussion Questions:

All jokes aside, was it right for Mrs. Nations to violate the law to advance a righteous cause?

Discussion Questions:

Mary Elizabeth Lease (1853–1933) was an American lecturer, writer, and political activist. She was an advocate of the suffrage movement as well as an advocate of temperance but she was best known for her work with the Populist Party. It is instructive that temperance was connected with other social causes: populism (a sort of 19th century Tea Party Movement) and the suffrage movement. Critics of Lease argued that she diluted her temperance work with tangential politics. Some WCTU members, Cary Nation for one, saw the temperance movement as the primary, and most holy calling, above all other social causes. Sometimes reformers hurt their main cause by joining tangential causes. Another example was Martin Luther King Jr. King was making great strides with Civil Rights legislation when he joined the anti-Vietnam War movement. He lost many supporters who thought he should stay focused on Civil Rights. What do you think? Do you think Lease and King were wrong to support equally important, but at times, contradictory social causes?

Discussion Questions:

Why did the mob prosper during Prohibition?

Discussion Questions:

Why is it impossible for a colorful crime figure like Al Capone to function in today's world?

Discussion Questions:

What was the defining moment when American education showed signs of decline?

Discussion Questions:

Pretend that you are a student in one of these schools. Keep a two-day diary where you describe all the things that happen.

Discussion Questions:

Many conservative Christians, Protestant and Roman Catholic, feel that Horace Mann did a great disservice to American education. Why?

Discussion Questions:

The author is obviously opposed to "government schools." What are some of his arguments?

Discussion Questions:

What did Moore and Holt write that influenced education in the United States?

Discussion Questions:

What are the three divisions of evangelicalism, and from what groups did they emerge?

Discussion Questions:

Compare British evangelicalism with American evangelicalism.

Discussion Questions:

How would you characterize yourself: Pentecostal, fundamentalist, or neo-evangelical?

Discussion Questions:

What is the primary argument in Mark Noll's book? Do you agree?

Discussion Questions:

Write a statement of your own theological beliefs.

Discussion Questions:

Why was the Scopes Trial so disastrous for America?

Discussion Questions:

If you were Williams Jennings Bryan, how would you have conducted this case differently?

Discussion Questions:

Why is a literal interpretation of the Creation story so important to Ham?

Discussion Questions:

William Jennings Bryan was one of the greatest Americans who ever lived. He was brilliant, hard working. He had a servant's heart, and he loved the Lord. Describe at least one other great Christian American who has had a great impact on this country.

Discussion Questions:

What advice does the author give evangelicals?

Discussion Questions:

Why was the rejection of the Weimar Republic, as laudable and just though it might be, the most natural thing in the world for Germany to do?

Discussion Questions:

Why did the Weimar Republic economy collapse?

Discussion Questions:

What effect did inflation have on Weimar Germany?

Discussion Questions:

Why was the cabaret the perfect place to dismantle a declining democracy and to plan a revolution?

Discussion Questions:

Germany in its moment of crisis turned from the best form of government to the worst because it felt threatened. What might America do if we were in a similar crisis?

Discussion Questions:

Germany, in its moment of crisis turned from the best form of government to the worst because it felt threatened. What might America do if we were in a similar crisis?

Discussion Questions:

How did the New Dealers differ from the Progressives?

Discussion Questions:

Offer evidence of the positive liberal state in the speech from today's lesson.

Discussion Questions:

What was the 1935 Social Security Act, and why was it necessary?

Discussion Questions:

What has been the result of social welfare?

Discussion Questions:

What criticism is Block speaking of in today's text?

Discussion Questions:

Recall one or two memorable events in the life of Mrs. Reynolds.

Discussion Questions:

The Church was a central part of most Depression era African-Americans. Why?

Discussion Questions:

Why didn't Mr. Calloway show more allegiance to the Northern army that would have promised him freedom?

Discussion Questions:

If you could ask Mr. Toler one question, what would that be?

Discussion Questions:

Based on all these accounts, how would you characterize slave-owners?

Discussion Questions:

Mrs. Cox wrote, "ended up in Algeria after having lived my whole life in Minnesota." Pretend you are the air force officer that she marries. Tell your story.

Discussion Questions:

Sergeant Melendrez says, "Every morning we'd attack (dawn attack) so by 3 or 4 in the afternoon we could set up for counter-attack. The squad leader in the evening would have a debriefing to get ready for the next attack. In the end there were only three guys left; I was getting scareder and scareder every day. Any guy who says he wasn't scared is lying. We weren't thinking about the job; we were thinking about staying alive." Why did Melendrez continue fighting?

Discussion Questions:

Mr. Manix says, "This was a major turning point in the war in the South Pacific." Mr. Manix thought, or wanted to think, that his campaign in New Guinea was the turning point of the war. It was an important campaign, but the allies had stopped the Japanese previously at Guadalcanal and the real turning point was at the Battle of Midway. Yet, Mr. Manix said this. Why?

Discussion Questions:

How did the media affect the life of Mr. Evans?

Discussion Questions:

Sergeant Alexander is putting his life on the line for all Americans, and he is the victim of racism. How does he feel?

Discussion Questions:

Define "Holocaust."

Discussion Questions:

Philosopher Hannah Arendt pointed out in her book *Origins of Totalitarianism* (1951), that Nazi Germany first deprived Jewish people of their citizenship and then it was free to deprive Jewish people of their human rights. Arendt underlined that in the Declaration of the Rights of Man and of the Citizen, citizens' rights actually preceded human rights, as the latter needed the protection of a determinate state to be actually respected. Why legally would it be impossible for such a thing to happen in England and the United States?

Discussion Questions:

From 1935 to 1942, why was European Jewry first defined and then localized into controlled communities?

Discussion Questions:

What problems does genocide present to the perpetrators and how are these overcome?

Discussion Questions:

How can it happen? How can the world produce a sane, even loving person like Eichmann who loves his children at night but murders millions of people in the daytime? What can we learn from this?

Discussion Questions:

How can it happen? How can the world produce a sane, even loving person like Eichmann who loves his children at night but murders millions of people in the daytime? What can we learn from this?

Discussion Questions:

Why did Russia and her former allies become enemies even before World War II ended?

Discussion Questions:

In what way was the Cold War a geopolitical conflict?

Discussion Questions:

What are the problems of fighting a limited war?

Discussion Questions:

Discuss what would have happened if America and the Soviet Union went to war over the Cuban Nuclear Crisis.

Discussion Questions:

Why did America enter the Vietnam War, and why did it lose the war?

Discussion Questions:

How reliable do you think Moses' account of this military incident is? Give reasons for your response.

Discussion Questions:

What was the subject matter of early silent movies?

Discussion Questions:

What impact did sound have on the movie-going experience?

Discussion Questions:

What is the compelling theme of *The Searchers*?

Discussion Questions:

The cinema technology has come full circle. From a silent movie with a common experience, to a talking film where each person quietly experiences the same film, to a satosphere where no one "sees or hears exactly the same movie." Predict what effect that this will have on American culture.

Discussion Questions:

What is unique about the origins of Rock 'n' Roll?

Discussion Questions:

Rock 'n' roll moved from African American protest music to mainstream, mostly white, music. How?

Discussion Questions:

In what way did rock 'n' roll become the first socially relevant music in America?

Discussion Questions:

Should Christians listen to rock 'n' roll?

Discussion Questions:

How were Barwick and her generation affected by Woodstock?

Discussion Questions:

Would you want to live in 1900? Why or why not?

Discussion Questions:

The human capacity for mass killing increased exponentially as a result of improved weaponry and the increased power of the state. The marriage of nationalism and technology has been fatal for mankind. The 20th century introduced new concepts: gulags, concentration camps, secret police, terrorism, genocide, and war. Why?

Discussion Questions:

Sociologist F. Fasick argues that youth culture is full of paradoxes. According to Fasick, adolescents face contradictory pulls from society. On the one hand, compulsory schooling keeps them socially and economically dependent on their parents. On the other hand, young people are encouraged to achieve some sort of independence in order to participate in the market economy of modern society. What sorts of problems will this inevitably create?

Discussion Questions:

What are the four problems that could sink America?

Discussion Questions:

What evidences do historians offer that progress in human rights was made in the 20th century?

Discussion Questions:

What is at least one sociological anomaly of the 1950s and 1960s?

Discussion Questions:

While consumer protection is a good idea, when could it go too far?

Discussion Questions:

In spite of great economic opportunity, why was the northern city a great disappointment to African Americans?

Discussion Questions:

How does Shelby Steele define "White Guilt"?

Discussion Questions:

Why did Saturday-morning television maintain heroes that were different from those in theaters?

Discussion Questions:

Why in certain governments do the definitions of government and state become blurred?

Discussion Questions:

Identify the types of governments of these nations:

China

Russia

USA

Vatican

England

France

Discussion Questions:

Federal and state officials combine efforts to fund education. Which of these statements is supported by this information?

A. Education is mainly a responsibility of private organizations.

B. Education by the state takes priority over federal regulations.

C. The federal government shares responsibility with the states for education.

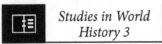

Discussion Questions:

President Nixon wanted to continue the war in Vietnam but Congress stopped him. How?

Discussion Questions:

The Supreme Court ruled that the Virginia Military Institute (VMI), an all-male college, had to admit women who meet their admission requirements. How did this ruling show that a public institution had discriminated against American citizens?

Discussion Questions:

Why, in your opinion, did America win the space race?

Discussion Questions:

No one can deny that von Braun was critical to the American space efforts. Indeed, the Russians would have probably beaten the Americans to the moon without von Braun. Yet, at the same time, no one can deny that von Braun was a war criminal. However, given the perceived crisis that existed in the Cold War, American officials chose to ignore von Braun's participation in the murder of thousands of Jewish and Russian slave laborers. Did the United States make the right choice?

Discussion Questions:

Ask your parents or grandparents what they were doing when the Challenger and the Columbia exploded.

Discussion Questions:

What challenges must be overcome before America can land a man on Mars?

Discussion Questions:

Is there alien life away from Earth? Why? Why not?

Discussion Questions:

Identify trends that are occurring in the modern family.

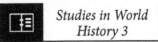
Discussion Questions:

Describe Blankenhorn's different types of fathers.

Discussion Questions:

What were the two sides that are emerging in the culture war surrounding American family life?

Discussion Questions:

Summarize Pastor William's exegesis of Galatians 3:28.

Discussion Questions:

What three modern questions does the mother ask that the man cannot answer?

Discussion Questions:

What theological challenges does the urban church face in the modern city?

Discussion Questions:

Urbanization has been very disorienting in the 20th century. Why?

Discussion Questions:

What challenges do modern cities face?

Discussion Questions:

What is a history maker?

Discussion Questions:

Why was the New Testament Antioch Church so special?

Discussion Questions:

n Post-Modernism there is no right or wrong, no doctrine. What implications can this have for a church?

Discussion Questions:

What are distinctives that exist in Post-Modern architecture?

Discussion Questions:

What are the problems with Post-Modern views of justice?

Discussion Questions:

Pretend that you are the youth director of your church. You must design an outreach to your Post-Modern world. What programs and interventions will you offer?

Discussion Questions:

What hopeful message does this author offer?

Discussion Questions:

Out of the four main food traditions in the United States, in which tradition does your family lie?

Discussion Questions:

How would you paraphrase what Chuck Colson is saying to contemporary Americans about love and pre-marital sex?

Discussion Questions:

What do you know about the Tea Party Movement?

Discussion Questions:

What are the causes of the 2008 Recession?

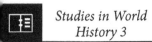
Discussion Questions:

Why is the author of this series cautiously optimistic about the future?

Discussion Questions:

What does Chambers mean in this statement? "Our Lord never takes measures to make me do what He wants."

Discussion Questions:

Lewis is writing an unsaved friend. What arguments does he offer to persuade his friend to commit his life to Christ?

Discussion Questions:

What does Merton mean in this statement? "The Christian must not only accept suffering: he must make
it holy."

Discussion Questions:

In what ways has Schaeffer's thinking changed?

Discussion Questions:

What does Mother Teresa mean in saying the following? "We are not social workers."

Discussion Questions:

Discuss the origin of the university.

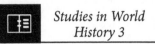

Discussion Questions:

On what grounds can a Christian argue that the American university was founded on Christian principles?

Discussion Questions:

What advice does the author have to Christians attending secular colleges?

Discussion Questions:

What is Pelikan's central thesis?

Discussion Questions:

What is the purpose of Harvard University in 1650?

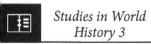
Discussion Questions:

Based upon today's text, why is hostage taking such an effective tactic against American interests?

Discussion Questions:

Why, in spite of an oil glut, have oil prices increased?

Discussion Questions:

What energy alternatives to oil consumption do Stobaugh and Yergin suggest?

Discussion Questions:

When does political violence increase, and who commits this violence?

Discussion Questions:

What are the four temptations that mankind faces? What is the Christian reponse?

Discussion Questions:

Why has European unity been so difficult?

Discussion Questions:

The term "United States of Europe," as a direct comparison with the United States of America, would imply that the existing nations of Europe would be reduced to a status equivalent to that of a U.S. state, losing their national sovereignty in the process and becoming constituent parts of a European federation. Just as the United States of America has evolved from a confederation (under the 1777 Articles of Confederation) into a federation, the term "the United States of Europe" implies that European countries will evolve into a federal republic. Do you think that this will occur? Is the comparison between the evolution of the United States of America and the European Union an accurate one?

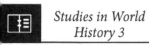

Discussion Questions:

Compare and contrast the American and European views of work.

Discussion Questions:

Would you rather live in Europe or America? Why?

Discussion Questions:

Rifkin's article is clearly anti-American. Explain.

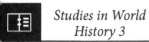
Discussion Questions:

Since the middle of the 17th century China has perceived itself as being in an adversarial role with the West. Why?

Discussion Questions:

In World War II, General Stillwell, in charge of American forces in China, lobbied Washington to channel some aid to the Communists; this was not because Stillwell was sympathetic to their cause but because the Communists was simply doing a better job fighting the Japanese than the Nationalists. Is war a time to suspend political ambitions and to support anyone, even an enemy, to defeat a greater enemy?

Discussion Questions:

Why do "people" movements, movements with laudable goals of "liberty, fraternity, and justice," eventually evolve into authoritarian regimes?

Discussion Questions:

In many nations persecution and poverty drive people to the Lord. In China it is prosperity. Explain.

Discussion Questions:

Do you believe that China will replace America as the premier economic power in the world?

Discussion Questions:

Do you believe that China will replace America as the premier economic power in the world?

Discussion Questions:

In what way is 21st-century terrorism different from earlier forms of terrorism?

Discussion Questions:

What ominous connection has existed from the beginning of terrorism?

Discussion Questions:

Why was terrorism employed more freely after World War II?

Discussion Questions:

How were the Sons of Liberty different from terrorist organizations of today?

Discussion Questions:

Do you agree with President Obama's assessment in 2009 that the War on Terrorism was over?

Discussion Questions:

What is a pandemic, and is AIDS a pandemic?

Discussion Questions:

Do you believe global warming is a problem?

Discussion Questions:

Do you share Warren Buffet's fears? Why?

Discussion Questions:

The problem with the overpopulation theory is that social liberals have used it as an excuse to promote immoral practices. Explain.

Discussion Questions:

Explain your eschatology.

Discussion Questions:

What do you think America will look like in 2030?

Discussion Questions:

Ken Sanes writes, "We live in a time in which the ability to create deceptive simulations, especially for television, has become essential to the exercise of power. And the inability to see through these deceptions has become a form of powerlessness. Those who let themselves be taken in by the multiple deceptions of politics, news, advertising and public relations, are doomed, like the more gullible member of the radio audience in 1938, to play a role in other people's dramas, while mistakenly believing that the are reacting to something genuine." Do you agree with Mr. Sanes' assessment?

Discussion Questions:

American author, Kurt Vonnegut, Jr., was fond of saying, "I don't write science fiction. I write non-fiction but it is so strange it seems like science fiction." Literary critic Bernard Crick writes, "If 1984 is treated as a warning rather than a prophecy, as a satire on present tendencies rather than a forecast of the future, it can be seen that its effect has been totally salutary. Today such terms as 'doublethink' 'newspeak' and 'thoughtcrime' have passed into accepted usage and for a generation of readers the book has come to be regarded as a standard treatise on the growth and influence of totalitarian trends." In what ways is Orwell's society like contemporary American society?

Discussion Questions:

Critic Peter Firchow writes, "For Huxley, it is plain, there is no need to travel into the future to find the brave new world; it already exists, only, too palpably, in the American Joy City, where the declaration of dependence begins and ends with the single-minded pursuit of happiness." Do you agree?

Discussion Questions:

Did you figure out the ending of this futuristic short story before reading the end? Write a fictional short story of what life would be like if the world was destroyed.

Chapter Exam Section

Fill in the blanks with words from the following list:

Avant-Garde

Epistemology

Moral Relativism

Pragmatism

Surrealism

1. _____ Philosophical view that argues for ordinary, common sense.

2. _____ The study of knowledge.

3. _____ Forward thinking, modern.

4. _____ Out of the real of ordinary experience.

5. _____ Morality based on circumstances.

Short Answer Essay:

In September 1976 I sat in Harvard University Chapel and heard Pastor Peter Gomes, the Harvard University Chaplain, tell us that we were the best of the best. The hope of America and the world. He told us to look around and see who the next president, governor, great author, and theologian would be. As one professor quipped, "There are those who go to Harvard, and those who don't." Why, on that day, should I, a born again, evangelical, be greatly concerned?

Fill in the blanks with words from the following list:

Margaret Sanger
"One Big Union for All"
Rough Riders
Social Gospel
Theodore Roosevelt

1. _____ A racist advocate of birth control.

2. _____ Was the goal of the radical labor leaders and Socialists who met in Chicago in 1905.

3. _____ A theory of helping the needy and poor based on human good, not the Bible.

4. _____ Great progressive president.

5. _____ Roosevelt's Spanish American troops who took San Juan Hill.

Short Answer Essay:

What disturbing trends emerged in the Progressive era media?

Fill in the blanks with words from the following list:

A constitutional monarchy

Dreadnoughts

Kulturkampf

Militarism

The Socialist Party

1. _____ Stuggles in culture.

2. _____ Large battleships thought to be unsinkable.

3. _____ Represented the middle class; became important in the German Empire.

4. _____ National philosophy of military power.

5. _____ In effect a democracy, and in Britain's case it also had a huge empire.

Short Answer Essay:

In 1914, Europe was experiencing significant progress in pure science and all the social sciences. It also included the most advanced civilizations in the world. This was a time of great hope and optimism. Apparently the Modernists had reason to be optimistic. Yet, in 1914, the worst war to date in human history began and dashed the hopes, and optimism, of everyone. Technology that previously was used to end poverty, to cure diseases, now invented poison gas and other barbaric weapons. Why did this happen?

Fill in the blanks with words from the following list:

Biplanes

Chaplain George T. McCarthy

Field hospitals

Lt. Col. George Brenton Laurie

Oswald Bölcke

1. _____ Joined the German Air Corps in 1914 and fought in every major engagement until he went missing in action in 1916.

2. _____ Early airplanes with dual wings that helped them maneuver.

3. _____ Emergency medical centers set up out where the battles ensued.

4. _____ From Nova Scotia; appointed a special service officer, including the command of a mounted infantry battalion for the South African War.

5. _____ Roman Catholic chaplain who made an effort to focus on the Lord in the midst of danger and death.

Short Answer Essay:

In spite of the fact that Modernism was in full swing by 1914, we find no evidence of Modern elitism, hope in science, and belief in the progress of man. On the contrary these memoirs and letters are very similar to war correspondence from the 17th and 18th century, from men and women who lived in an entirely different era. Are these men and women anomalies, or are they really not affected by the temper of the times?

Fill in the blanks with words from the following list:

Mass communication

Morrill Act

Neurasthenia

Vaudeville

Yellow journalism

1. _____ A form of comedy entertainment.

2. _____ National anxiety.

3. _____ Federal act to set up lend lease colleges.

4. _____ Forms of media that reach a broad, national audience.

5. _____ Sensational, salacious writings to persuade an audience to buy into a lie.

Short Answer Essay:

I hate my computer. Yuck! Just as soon as I halfway understand a windows platform they change it. Where is Windows 98 when you need it! I mean peanut butter is the same forever; why can't computers stay the same? And, to make matters worse, my son persuaded me to buy a MAC. A what? A MAC! The darn thing has a delete key that moves to the left instead of to the right. What is wrong with a world that creates a computer that has a delete key that moves to the left instead of the right? I share the misgivings of one of my least favorite philosophers, existentialist Martin Heidegger. What Heidegger called "the essence of technology" infiltrates human existence more intimately than anything humans could create. The danger of technology lies in the transformation of the human being, by which human actions and aspirations are fundamentally distorted. Not that machines can run amok, or even that we might misunderstand ourselves through a faulty comparison with machines. Instead, technology enters the inmost recesses of human existence, transforming the way we know and think and will. Technology is, in essence, a dehumanizing influence by humanizing us ! Heidegger died in 1976, long before the personal computer and computer networks, such as the Web, much less digital viewers, etc., became a reality. However, as early as 1957 Heidegger foresaw the computer, what he called the "language machine." But it is no such thing—the computer creates no language at all. It creates symbols that are meaningless. FYI KWIM (For your information, know what I mean? DUMMY!). My son Peter and his generation—that is your generation—think that man is the master of the language machine. But the truth of the matter is that the language machine takes language into its management and thus masters the essence of the human being. (Portions are quoted from http://www.regent.edu/). What advantages, if any, do technology bring Americans?

Fill in the blanks with words from the following list:

Bolshevism

Crew of Battleship *Potemkin*

Czar Nicholas II

Duma

Lenin

1. _____ Russian participants in the 1905 Revolution.
2. _____ Czar when the Russian Revolution arrived.
3. _____ The Russian Parliament.
4. _____ Leader of the Russian Revolution.
5. _____ Russian Communism.

Short Answer Essay:

The roots of communism's ultimate failure were evident even in 1917. What were these failures?

Fill in the blanks with words from the following list:

18th Amendment

Nativist

Prohibition

The Woman's Christian Temperance Union (WCTU)

Volstead Act

1. _____ Outlawed the sale of alcohol products in the United States.

2. _____ A group who opposed immigration of all sorts.

3. _____ Banning the production and sale of alcohol.

4. _____ Defined intoxicating beverages as anything with more than 0.5 percent alcohol.

5. _____ Organized by women concerned about the destructive power of alcohol.

Short Answer Essay:

American in 1917 overwhelmingly supported Prohibition. In 1919, a year before Prohibition went into effect, Cleveland had 1,200 legal bars. All were closed. In 4 years, though, by 1923, the city had an estimated 3,000 illegal speakeasies, along with 10,000 stills. An estimated 30,000 city residents sold liquor during Prohibition, and another 100,000 made home brew or bathtub gin for themselves and friends. Why?

Fill in the blanks with words from the following list:

Homeschooling

Horace Mann

John Holt

Raymond Moore

Unschooling

1. _____ A movement that has existed through all of American history but has become more popular since the 1970s.

2. _____ Early leader in public education.

3. _____ Pioneer in home education.

4. _____ Educator who was critical of orthodox education.

5. _____ The educational philosophy of John Holt's followers; what he called "learning by living."

Short Answer Essay:

Predict the future of public education.

Fill in the blanks with words from the following list:

Crucicentrism

Harold Ockenga

John Wesley

Jonathan Edwards

Second Great Awakening

1. _____ The great revival in American in the 19th century.
2. _____ A great evangelist who founded Fuller Seminary.
3. _____ Cross-centered theology.
4. _____ The founder of Methodism.
5. _____ American philosopher and theologian.

Short Answer Essay:

Predict the future of American evangelicalism.

Fill in the blanks with words from the following list:

American Civil Liberties Union

Butler Act

Clarence Darrow

National Stumping

William Jennings Bryan

1. _____ Tennessee law that made the teaching of evolution illegal.

2. _____ A private liberal organization devoted to upholding the Constitution.

3. _____ The successful lawyer at the Scopes Trial.

4. _____ A great American statesman.

5. _____ To hold informal mass rallies in support of a position or ideology.

Short Answer Essay:

The so-called Scopes Monkey Trial in Dayton, Tennessee, was a watershed moment in the history of this country. The ramifications of those proceedings are still being felt today. Marvin Olasky and John Perry in their book *Monkey Business: True Story of the Scopes Trial* argue that the courtroom drama was not the real story. The media's handling of the drama really is the story. This court case was made sensational just like the O. J. Simpson Trial, by the media. The way the entire event was conducted and perceived by the rest of the nation set the tone for how creationists and evolutionists have been viewed by society ever since. Most people have a misunderstanding of what happened based on slanted newspaper reporting accounts of H. L. Menken, who made fun of creationists, and by radio announcers who did the same. As a result, the case for creationism has been crippled in the eyes of society. What can we do today to offer an alternative, truthful story of what happened? And then, how can we influence a society that already has its mind made up?

Fill in the blanks with words from the following list:

German Reich

McCarthy Era

Protective Tariffs

Reparation

Weimar Republic

1. _____ A period of German democracy after WWI and before the Nazis took power.

2. _____ A German government.

3. _____ Money paid as punishment for the loss of a war.

4. _____ Duties placed on goods to protect indigenous industries.

5. _____ A time of heightened fear against Communism in the United States.

Short Answer Essay:

From the start, the Weimar Republic was deeply troubled. When the constitution was first established, many Germans were highly suspicious of the new government, and extremists on the left and right rejected the authority of the Weimar Republic, undermining its effectiveness. While the government was theoretically a coalition comprised of numerous political parties, it was attacked on all sides. In other words, it was a great government, perhaps the best government in world history, but disliked by everyone. In retrospect, would it have been better to have a more autocratic government, or a socialist government (the opposite extreme)? At least one group would take ownership of the government—the Weimar Republic was an orphan loved by no one. With one strong group, perhaps alliances could have been built with other groups. What do you think?

Fill in the blanks with words from the following list:

Great Depression

Herb Block

National Recovery Administration

Positive Liberal State

Public Works Administration

The New Deal

1. _____ A time of great economic stress, 1929-1940.

2. _____ Roosevelt's legislation intervention.

3. _____ A state with a lot of government intervention.

4. _____ A New Deal agency committed to oversight of labor and management.

5. _____ Job creation agency in the New Deal.

6. _____ A political cartoonist.

Short Answer Essay:

Suggest an alternative to the New Deal.

Fill in the blanks with words from the following list:

Ben Horry

Federal Writers' Project (FWP)

John A. Lomax

Mary Reynolds

Walter Calloway

. _____ Sent writers into 17 states to interview ordinary people in order to write down their life stories.

. _____ National Advisor on Folklore and Folkways for the FWP.

. _____ Born in slavery to the Kilpatrick family, she claimed to be more than a hundred years old.

. _____ Lived to be 89, with most of his life spent on the south side of Birmingham.

. _____ From Murrells Inlet, South Carolina, and told his account of slavery.

Short Answer Essay:

Based on all these accounts, how would you characterize slave-owners?

Fill in the blanks with words from the following list:

Andrew Melendrez

Carlisle Evans

John William Manix

Leona Cox

The Nuclear Age

1. _____ A period that of nuclear power that gained prominence at the end of World War II.

2. _____ A Red Cross nurse during World War II.

3. _____ Sergeant in the US Army fighting in Europe during World War II.

4. _____ Fought with the US Army in the Pacific.

5. _____ Fought with the Marines in the Pacific.

Short Answer Essay:

What are advantages and disadvantages of using oral history?

Fill in the blanks with words from the following list:

Anti-Semitism

Einsatzgruppen

Final Solution

Ghettoization

Gleichschaltung

Holocaust

Mischlinge

National Socialist government

Nuremberg Laws of 1935

Wannsee Conference

1. _____ Systematic prejudice against Jewish people.

2. _____ Murder of millions Jews during World War II.

3. _____ Nazi government.

4. _____ A German designation for a Jewish person.

5. _____ Determined who was Jewish and who was not.

6. _____ Take over by Nazis of the civil services.

7. _____ Mobile killing units in Russia.

8. _____ Placing Jews in containment areas for later deportation.

9. _____ German plan to kill all the Jews in Europe.

10. _____ A German conference to deal with the extermination of the Jews.

Short Answer Essay:

One of the reasons, Hilberg explains, that Germany ultimately created the Holocaust was that most nations, including the United States, only accepted a limited number of Jewish immigrants. Why?

Fill in the blanks with words from the following list:

Geopolitical Conflict

Iron Curtain

Limited War

Vietnamization

Winston Churchill

. _____ A metaphor for the closing of the borders between free, democratic Europe and Soviet controlled Eastern Europe.

. _____ A world-wide conflict between two different political ideologies.

. _____ As opposed to limited war, combatants intentionally limit the extent and scope of warfare.

. _____ An attempt by the Americans to leave the conduct of the War to South Vietnam.

. _____ British prime minister during World War II.

Short Answer Essay:

Why was the Cold War such an unusual war?

Fill in the blanks with words from the following list:

Daguerreotype

Phenakistiscope

Thaumatrope

Tom Mix

Vitascope

1. _____ A card with different pictures on either side so that when the card is rapidly twirled, the images appear to combine.

2. _____ An early animation device that used the persistence of vision principle to create an illusion of motion.

3. _____ The first commercially successful photographic process.

4. _____ An early film projector first demonstrated in 1895.

5. _____ Early cinema cowboy star.

Short Answer Essay:

The single most significant new instrument of mass entertainment was the movies. Movie attendance rose 50 million a week in 1920 to 90 million weekly in 1929. Americans spent 83 cents of every entertainment dollar going to the movies, and three-fourths of the population went to a movie theater every week. During the late teens and 1920s, the film industry took on its modern form. By the 1920s, the industry had relocated to Hollywood. Each year, Hollywood released nearly 700 movies, dominating worldwide film production. What implications/effects did this have on American culture?

Fill in the blanks with words from the following list:

Blues

Dixieland

Jazz

Ragtime

Rock 'n' Roll

1. _____ A type of music emerging in the 1950s.

2. _____ The name given to both a musical form and a music genre that originated in African-American communities of primarily the "Deep South" of the United States.

3. _____ A musical style that originated at the beginning of the 20th century in African American communities in the Southern United States.

4. _____ An original musical genre that enjoyed its peak popularity between 1900 and 1918.

5. _____ Sometimes referred to as Hot jazz, Early Jazz or New Orleans jazz, this is a style of jazz music that developed in New Orleans at the start of the 20th century.

Short Answer Essay:

Interview parents or other adult relatives or friends. Develop questions relating to rock's influence on the interviewee and whether or not that person has ever been involved in social protest.

Fill in the blanks with words from the following list:

20th-century movement

Concentration camps

Scientific Revolution

Social Revolution

Youth Culture

1. _____ Dynamic changes in family, government, and society.

2. _____ A term that describes the growing influence of youth.

3. _____ Dynamic changes in technological progress, including fields of medicine and media.

4. _____ The nation's population shifted from the Northeast to the Sunbelt.

5. _____ Massive prison-holding facilities often used to slaughter large groups of people.

Short Answer Essay:

World history is often written as a series of wars, large conflicts that stem from leaders who imagine that everyone would be better off if they won a war. The language these leaders us include, "if I owned that land," "if they used our political policy," or "if only the superior race existed." Historian Jay Winter in his book *Dreams of Peace and Freedom: Utopian Moments in the Twentieth Century* (2006. Yale Press: New Haven, Connecticut) has termed these events "major utopias," ideas that "uproot, cleanse, transform, exterminate." Winter focuses on six moments when, following a major event, people were able to reflect on the past and imagine a better future. Following the Great War, President Woodrow Wilson posited that self-determination, the ability of a country to determine its own political future, would bring an end to international conflict. In 1937, on the verge of another war, the World's Fair in Paris presented technology as the vehicle of peace, an idea shattered with the advent of the atomic bomb. The social movements of the 20th century are marked by the signing of the Universal Declaration of Human Rights in 1948. These movements continued into the 1960s, a period marked by the liberation of people everywhere, mostly through peaceful uprisings. Finally, the 1990s brought the concept of global citizenship, that individuals can think of themselves as the object of change, to end "poverty, oppression, humiliation, and collective violence. These benchmarks of progress exhibit great optimism. Do you share his optimism about the future? If you do, what "utopias" are waiting to happen?

Fill in the blanks with words from the following list:

Black Nationalism

Ghettoization

Racism

Ralph Nader

White Guilt

. _____ An early leader of the consumer movement.

. _____ A term to describe the movement of African-Americans into poor sections of the city.

. _____ African-American movement that celebrated African-American exclusionism.

. _____ A term to describe guilt over racial relations.

. _____ A belief system based on the concept that people are divided into races, and that certain races are superior to others.

Short Answer Essay:

Shelby Steele wrote a short book, *A Bound Man: Why We are Excited about Obama and Why He Can't Win*, published in December 2007. The book contained Steele's analysis of Barack Obama's character as a child born to a mixed couple who then has to grow as a black man." Steele then concludes that Barack Obama is a "bound man" to his "black identity." Steele gives this description of his conclusion: "There is a price to be paid even for fellow-traveling with a racial identity as politicized and demanding as today's black identity. This identity wants to take over a greater proportion of the self than other racial identities do. It wants to have its collective truth— its defining ideas of grievance and protest—become personal truth. . . . These are the identity pressures that Barack Obama lives within. He is vulnerable to them because he has hungered for a transparent black identity much of his life. He needs to 'be black.' And this hunger—no matter how understandable it may be—means that he is not in a position to reject the political liberalism inherent in his racial identity. For Obama liberalism is blackness." Do you agree with Steele's assessment?

Fill in the blanks with words from the following list:

Executive Branch

Federal government of the United States

Government

Judicial Branch

Legislative Branch

1. _____ Composed of the president and his cabinet.

2. _____ Congress and its influence.

3. _____ The court system.

4. _____ Composed of the executive branch, the legislative branch, and the judicial branch.

5. _____ Refers to the way people arbitrate, control, and live their lives.

Short Answer Essay:

Under President Dr. Charles S. MacKenzie, the college was the plaintiff-appellee in the landmark U.S. Supreme Court case in 1984, Grove City College v. Bell. The ruling came seven years after the school's refusal to sign a Title IX compliance form, which would have subjected the entire school to federal regulations, even future ones not yet issued. Without researching what happened, predict the outcome.

Fill in the blanks with words from the following list:

Apollo

Gemini

Mercury Project

Sputnik

Wernher Von Braun

1. _____ Early NASA efforts to put a man in space.

2. _____ Russian satelitte—the first one in space.

3. _____ NASA efforts to understand space travel.

4. _____ NASA efforts to go to the moon.

5. _____ Former Nazi German space scientist who helped the Americans.

Short Answer Essay:

The United States Space Program had its origins in the missile-based arms race that occurred just after the end of World War II, with both the Soviet Union and the United States capturing advanced German Nazi rocket technology and personnel. It was motivated by the Cold War desire to display scientific and technological prowess, which translated into military hegemony. Between 1957 and 1977, the rivalry between the two nations became focused on space exploration. The Space Race effectively began with the Soviet launch of the Sputnik 1 satellite on October 4, 1957, and it concluded with the co-operative Apollo-Soyuz Test Project human spaceflight mission in July 1975, which came to symbolize peace between the USA and USSR. The United States committed themselves to the Space Shuttle program that wound down in the second decade of the 21st century. The next goal is the exploration of and landing on Mars. Will that happen in your lifetime? Is space travel over?

Fill in the blanks with words from the following list:

Fatherhood

Feminism

Galatians 3:28

Leave it to Beaver

Traditional family

1. _____ A successful sitcom television show in the 1950s.

2. _____ An assertive women's rights movement.

3. _____ A movement to save fathers' roles in families.

4. _____ A typical family from the 1960s that comprised a working father, a homemaker mother, and their two kids.

5. _____ Biblical passage that speaks of the equal status of all who are in Christ.

Short Answer Essay:

The Ozzie and Harriet 1950s television series was one of the most popular in world history. Discuss why such a show today would not be popular.

Fill in the blanks with words from the following list:

Antioch Church

City of God, City of Satan

History Maker

Skyscraper

Urbanization

1. _____ Terms coined to describe a notion that Satan wants to own the city.

2. _____ A movement in history toward a majority of world dwellers living in the city.

3. _____ A term to describe someone who really changes history.

4. _____ A city church that welcomed diversity of all types.

5. _____ Tall buildings to accommodate the maximum number of people within a minimum space.

Short Answer Essay:

Pretend that you are pastoring an inner-city, cathedral church. Your church has declined in membership consistently for 20 years. In fact you now have 30 members. But, at the same time, your endowment has grown to 30 million dollars. What can you do to turn your church around?

Fill in the blanks with words from the following list:

Grant Wacker

Immanuel Kant

Post-modern architecture

Post-Modernism

Richard Rorty

1. _____ Post-1990 movement that emphasizes the subjective.
2. _____ A philosopher who emphasized the use of language.
3. _____ A philosopher who saw experience as the primary core reality.
4. _____ Created new designs and new visions in buildings.
5. _____ Insists that the growth of the Church has, and must, employ whatever tools God provides — including the media.

Short Answer Essay:

Why is Post-Modernism such a great threat to the Judeo-Christian Modern family?

Fill in the blanks with words from the following list:

Distinctive food

Edward Gibbon

Free market capitalists

Recession of 2008

Tea Party Movement

- _____ A conservative political movement whose main purpose is to decrease government control of American life.

- _____ The most serious economic downturn since the Great Depression.

- _____ Became a defining symbol of national identity in the 19th century.

- _____ Assert that government intervention merely drags out recessions and depressions.

- _____ Author of *The Decline and Fall of the Roman Empire*.

Short Answer Essay:

In 2012 Christian leader Chuck Colson wrote, "We have come to the point—I say this very soberly—when if there isn't a dramatic change is circumstances, we as Christians may well be called upon to stand in civil disobedience against the actions of our own government. That would break my heart as a former Marine Captain loving my country, but I love my God more... I've made up my mind—sober as that decision would have to be—that I will stand for the Lord regardless of what my state tells me." Do you think it has gotten that bad in America?

Fill in the blanks with words from the following list:

Clive Staples (C.S.) Lewis

Francis Schaeffer

Mother Teresa

Oswald Chambers

Thomas Merton

1. _____ Early 20th-century saint who wrote a very popular devotional *My Utmost for His Highest.*

2. _____ Professor of Medieval and Renaissance English literature at Cambridge University.

3. _____ One of the most influential American spiritual writers of the 20th century.

4. _____ Moved to Switzerland in 1948 as a missionary, and founded L'Abri (the Shelter) Fellowship with his wife, Edith.

5. _____ Her Missionaries of Charity grew from 12 to thousands serving the "poorest of the poor" in 450 centers around the world.

Short Answer Essay:

List the five most Christians leaders of the 20th century. Why did you make these choices?

Fill in the blanks with words from the following list:

Christo et Ecclesiae

Harvard University Charter

King Belshazzar's Feast

University

University of Bologna

1. _____ The first university.

2. _____ A metaphor based on the Book of Daniel to explain the university.

3. _____ A charter stating the mission and purpose of Harvard University.

4. _____ An institution of advanced education and research that grants academic degrees.

5. _____ Harvard's motto for 300 years, which meant "for Christ and church."

Short Answer Essay:

Will you attend a secular or a Christian university? Why?

Fill in the blanks with words from the following list:

Assassination

Iranian Hostages

Oil Crisis

Robert Stobaugh

T. S. Eliot

1. _____ The Iran hostage crisis was a diplomatic crisis between Iran and the United States where 52 Americans were held hostage for 444 days from November 4, 1979, to January 20, 1981.

2. _____ Shortages of oil that caused spiked oil prices.

3. _____ Author of *Future Energy*.

4. _____ Murder of a political official.

5. _____ Perhaps the best poet and dramatist of the 20th century.

Short Answer Essay:

Discuss one important story that is on page 2, behind the headlines!

Fill in the blanks with words from the following list:

Common Market

European Parliament

European Union

Jeremy Rifkin

United States of Europe

1. _____ The union of continental Europe after the Iron Curtain fell in 1990.

2. _____ The governing body of the European Union.

3. _____ A controversial New Left historian.

4. _____ A term used by Victor Hugo during a speech at the International Peace Congress in 1849.

5. _____ Advances free trade and uniform standards.

Short Answer Essay:

What danger, if any, does an EU pose to America? Why is America slow to recognize EU's potential?

Fill in the blanks with words from the following list:

Chiang Kaishek

Great Leap Forward

Mao Zedong

Manchus

Tiananmen Square

. _____ Late 19th-century ruling Chinese family.

. _____ Historical gathering place of radicals and revolutionaries.

. _____ Nationalist leader of China.

. _____ Communist leader of Chinia.

. _____ Economic and social revolution in the 1960s.

Short Answer Essay:

Should America attempt to promote democracy in China? Or should we merely do business with it?

Fill in the blanks with words from the following list:

Collateral Damage

Jewish Zealots

Religious extremists

Sons of Liberty

Terrorism

1. _____ Systematic violence against a government on behalf of a cause.

2. _____ Injury to non-combatant civilians.

3. _____ Radical Jewish Zionists who sought freedom for Israel.

4. _____ Often view modernization efforts as corrupting influences on traditional culture.

5. _____ Organized into patriotic chapters as a result of the Stamp Tax of 1765.

Short Answer Essay:

When, if ever, is terrorism justifiable?

Fill in the blanks with words from the following list:

Eschatology

Global Warming

Pandemic

Parousia

Premillennialism

1. _____ A worldwide disease epidemic.

2. _____ A theory that the world is warming.

3. _____ Study of the end times.

4. _____ The Second Coming of Jesus Christ.

5. _____ A belief of the end times held by a large percentage of Christians during the first three centuries of the Christian era.

Short Answer Essay:

Offer some biblical reasons why you should not fear the future.

Fill in the blanks with words from the following list:

Fortress Nation

Futurology

Globalized World

Hindenburg

Orson Welles

1. _____ The prediction of the future.

2. _____ A world who draws its vision and resources from the entire globe.

3. _____ A concept of a world that is paraochial and self-serving.

4. _____ Gave a live performance of H.G. Wells' science fiction novel *The War of the Worlds*.

5. _____ The German passenger zeppelin airship that caught fire and was destroyed in 1937.

Short Answer Essay:

Are the fears and nightmares of Huxley and Orwell coming true today?

Answer Key

━● Discussion Question Answer Key

Chapter 1

Lesson 1

Modernism basically said, "You will embrace my new thing, you will be open, free, and tolerant, or I will destroy you." Modernism became the thing it despised. Likewise, it rejected religion only to produce a surrogate religion in its place.

Lesson 2

It represented the best that mankind could overcome the most arduous obstacle created by God and nature. It showed, too, that elusive unity was indeed possible.

Lesson 3

Eliot's poem "The Cocktail Party" with its self-reflection and melancholy capture well the dreariness and trepidation that is so much a part of Modernism. Browning, on the other hand, a romantic, ably captures the subjective, warm feelings of companionship and love.

Lesson 4

Modern thinkers doomed themselves to repeat the same errors of previous generations because they refused to learn from history. History to Modernism was therapeutic or entertaining, but not didactic. Thus, modern and abstract art grew as tyrannical about its unpredictable lines and composition that it began to mirror earlier tyrannical artistic movements of the Middle Ages. Likewise, Modernism in general is completely unable to learn form its mistakes and refuses to value other perspectives.

Lesson 5

Answers will vary. Surely mankind should learn not to rely on technology and science to protect us from all things. God alone is omnipotent and omnipresent.

Chapter 2

Lesson 1

In modern society, among Progressives in particular, there was a growing mistrust of common people to know what was good for them. Social policy, as in art, "professionals" sought to control the personal habits of Americans, for, in their eyes, the most laudable of reasons. Progressives were not intentionally bad, but their patronizing, "big brother" attitudes would have disastrous effects on western society.

Lesson 2

One historian explains, "Croly, like most Progressives, was convinced that only a public-spirited, disinterested elite, guided by scientific principles, could restore the promise of American life. Thus, he called for the establishment of government regulatory commissions, staffed by independent experts, to protect American democracy from the effects of corporate power. He also believed that human nature 'can be raised to a higher level by an improvement in institutions and laws.' According to Croly, the challenge confronting early 20th century America was to respond to the problems that had accompanied the transformation of American society from a rural, agricultural culture into an urban, industrial society. Filled with faith in the power of government, Progressives launched reform in the areas of public health, housing, urban planning and design, parks and recreation, workplace safety, workers compensation, pensions, insurance, poor relief, and health care." www.digitalhistory.uh.edu.

Lesson 3

Overall, it is fairly accurate. If anything the newsboys were much worse than the movie portrayed. Plus, the New York World did not really cave into the demands, although many reforms resulted directly and indirectly from the strike.

Lesson 4

Roosevelt was a new kind of president: a charismatic, articulate, compassionate, heroic leader, who sought to improve every aspect of society. He made the presidency as large as the problems posed by industrialization and urbanization. The people loved him! He was larger than life. No longer would America elect the moody, congenial, but very ugly Abraham Lincoln-type president.

Lesson 5

The obvious problem is that a small minority of Americans pay all the taxes. Another problem was unanticipated: as more and more Americans grew dependent upon the dole, and other social welfare benefits, the income tax return was the vehicle that the government used to dispense benefits, and, at the same time, gain more control over American lives. It also hard to hold the federal government accountable for the vast tax revenue it collected: enormous amounts of federal taxes were wasted. Other revenue was used for partisan, selfish purposes.

Chapter 3

Lesson 1

The Austrian Empire was well on its way to becoming a second-rate power yet its Emperor refused to admit this and insisted on maintaining its dominance over at least the lowly Balkans. Thus, when the Archduke of Austria was assassinated, Austria used it as an excuse to declare war on the Serbs. Serbia was aligned with Russia who declared war on Austria. Germany was allied with Austria so that meant war between Germany and Russia. Russia had a treaty with France so war with Russia meant war with France and war with France who had a treaty with England, meant war with England. The world, in macabre irony, caught in its own trap, went to war.

Lesson 2

In the last century, the concept of "myth" was developed extensively by a sociologist named Joseph Campbell. Campbell often described mythology as having four functions: to deal with the metaphysical (spiritual) world, to explain the shape of the universe, to validate and to explain the existing social order, to guide individuals through the stages of life. Campbell believed that if myths are to work in our modern world, they must continually evolve because the older mythologies, untransformed, simply do not address the realities of contemporary life, particularly with regard to the changing cosmological and sociological realities of each new era. Thus, quite simply, the myths that were promulgated by Modernism—inevitable progress, elitism, faith in science—could not cut the mustard in World War I. Newsflash: the same sort of thing is happening today and that is where you, young people, come in. You need to create a new set of myths, based on the Word of God, that will sustain Americans in the future!

Lesson 3

Germany, the most powerful force in Central Europe could have, should have, been a stabilizing force among its volatile and unstable weak neighbors (Austro-Hungary and Russia). But it was not. In fact, it more or less issued a blank check to its weak allies and they cashed the check and ushered in World War I.

Lesson 4

In 1914 Europe thought of war as an extension of foreign policy. Short, effective wars had effectively advanced national interests for a millennium. World War I, at the beginning, it was imagined by most, would be another splendid war full of low casualties, colorful flags and stirring charges, and stories of valor for all to tell their grandchildren. The problem was that military hardware had superseded military strategy. The same thing had occurred in the American Civil War where the rifle and rifled canon killed one out of five combatants. The American soldier lined up in neat rows and was slaughtered. This worked in the American Revolution when the inaccurate musket and smooth bore canon was used. It was disastrous in the American Civil War.

But that was America and this was Europe, and it was really shocking, that European military planners did not pick up on this. The problem was the machine gun, originally invented by the Germans. This nasty machine could kill 50-60 men in one minute. This was not war; this was slaughter.

Lesson 5

The governments in Europe, even the democratic governments, were fairly ineffective in diplomacy and politics. Modernism and Progressivism had disoriented governments and they were ill prepared to handle the crisis that occurred in June 1914. Socialism, Bolshevism, and Anarchy, in particular, had weakened European governments and they simply could not effectively defuse the crisis that exploded in the Balkans. In spite of the liberal, nationalist revolutions of the past one-half century, very few of the countries of Europe were democracies. It is hard for a democracy to go to war because the people (not just an individual ruler or small group of ministers) need to agree to go to war. The autocracies, monarchies, needed no such popular support.

Chapter 4

Lesson 1

To have a loved one missing in action in many ways was worse than having him killed. There was no closure.

Lesson 2

No. The Modernist, Brock, is trying to remove the religious tone of this young soldier's writing. He was an artist. But he saw God and God's Providence in all things. Thus, he was not a "skeptic" enamored with Goethe and Beethoven. This young man was a Child of God, born again, in love with Jesus. His peace was not bestowed by God. No, he is not lost, nor is the universe to him anything. But he knows he has a mansion in heaven!

Lesson 3

Answers will vary. I might first simply listen and let her tell me her struggles. I would avoid pretending that I knew anything about what she experienced. However, I would affirm the goodness of God in the midst of suffering and pain.

Lesson 4

No one knows for sure, but, based on this diary, Lt. Colonel Laurie was the type of officer who chose to reject the special privileges of his rank, choosing instead to share the hardships and struggles of those soldiers under his command - whether that meant lack of food or dangerous conditions. He could have lived in safety behind the lines. He chose not to do that. He put himself in harm's way from the moment he arrived on the Western Front.

Lesson 5

War encourages us to keep what is important important and to ignore that which is not.

Chapter 5

Lesson 1

Newspapers, in particular, were cheap. And in order to turn profit editors had to publish news reports and editorials that appealed to as wide an audience as possible. At first this spawned a sort of objectivity. The so-called penny press wanted to appeal to everyone's interest and thus, logically, it stood opposed to anyone's "special" interest—except of course its own interests, which presumably corresponded to its expressed policy of indifference (Fang 52). It wasn't long though before journalists discovered a truism that corrupted modern media forever: the fact is Americans would buy most anything if it included sensational, salacious, interest facts.

Lesson 2

Amusement parks were generally a good thing for America. They invited families to enjoy things together at an affordable price. In the long run, though, amusement parks whet the appetites of Americans and caused them to want more and more sensational experiences. Ultimately, in the 1950s, television moved entertainment and leisure into homes and families more or less spent less time enjoying a community experience. Television is an individual experience where each participant enjoys the media by himself.

Lesson 3

Answers will vary. More and more Americans, especially older Americans, are disoriented by advances in technology and are, in effect rejecting new technologies. For instance, I refused to buy an iPhone for many years because I was afraid I would not know how to use it.

Lesson 4

American universities proliferated over the country. The Morrill Act made sure that every state would have at last a state university. Pedagogy changed. At the same time the concept of "graduate school" emerged. Modeled on German universities, these institutions did not simply train undergraduates. They also provided graduate and professional training in law, medicine, engineering, and divinity. Suddenly, too, the "elective" was offered. The elective system made universities more attractive to a broader range of students and expanded the skills that they acquired.

Lesson 5

Answers will vary.

Chapter 6

He should have stopped World War I, granted vast amounts of freedoms to his people, turned over power to the Duma, and left Russia!

Lesson 2

Arguably World War I was the cause of the Russian Revolution. In many ways Russia's disastrous participation in World War I was the final blow to Czarist rule. The spirit of the nation was broken. Czar Nicholas made no serious attempt to reform his autocratic policies and the people rebelled.

Lesson 3

In a Democracy citizens have certain liberties and freedoms, which are protected by the constitution. In communism private ownership is not allowed whereas in democracy it is allowed. Communism is a socio economic system that stands for the establishment of a classless, egalitarian, and stateless society. Democracy is a political system of governance carried out by either the people directly or by elected representatives. In communism, power is vested in a group of people who decide the course of action. Democracy is a rule by the people and the elected representatives are bound to fulfill the wishes of the society.

Lesson 4

Clearly with the Bolsheviks. Reed died in 1920. I wonder if Reed would have changed his mind after the bloody civil war that raged for four years. I wonder if he would have changed his mind if he saw Stalin in the 1930s murder millions (quite literally millions) of his citizens. In fact, Stalin's 1930 purge killed double the number of victims who died in the Holocaust.

Lesson 5

Communism was not just a threat to capitalism. It was a threat to Christianity. But, at the same time, King hoped that both the Church, and capitalism, would not dilute the righteousness of its position by participating in unjust racism. King said, "Wherever the early Christians went, they made a triumphant witness for Christ. Whether on the village streets or in the city jails, they daringly proclaimed the good news of the gospel. Their reward for this audacious witness was often the excruciating agony of a lion's den or the poignant pain of a chopping block, but they continued in the faith that they had discovered a cause so great and had been transformed by a Savior so divine that even death was not too great a sacrifice. When they entered a town, the power structure became disturbed. Their new gospel brought the refreshing warmth of spring to men whose lives had been hardened by the long winter of traditionalism. They urged men to revolt against old systems of injustice and old structures of immorality. When the rulers objected, these strange people, intoxicated with the wine of God's grace, continued to proclaim the gospel until even men and women in Caesar's household were convinced, until rulers dropped their keys, and until kings trembled on their thrones. T. R. Glover has written that the early Christians 'out-thought, out-lived, and out-died' everyone else. Where is that kind of fervor today? Where is that kind of daring, revolutionary commitment to Christ today? Is it hidden behind smoke screens and altars? Is it buried in a grave called respectability? Is it inextricably bound with nameless status quos and imprisoned within cells of stagnant mores? This devotion must again be released. Christ must once more be enthroned in our lives. This is our best defense against Communism."

Chapter 7

Lesson 1

Prohibition failed because it was unenforceable. By 1925, half a dozen states, including New York, passed laws banning local police from investigating violations.

Nonetheless, it worked. The death rate from alcoholism was cut by 80 percent. Still, in 1927, there were an estimated 30,000 illegal speakeasies—twice the number of legal bars before Prohibition. Many people made beer and wine at home. It was relatively easy finding a doctor to sign a prescription for medicinal whiskey. In short, in ten years Americans had changed its mind about alcohol consumption. It had, in effect, had a failure of nerve. Marijuana use leads to more significant drug use.

Lesson 2

Since no one was hurt, it seemed to be acceptable. On the other hand, it was a distraction from the main issue: prohibition. No one knows, however, how/if her actions influenced Congress and then the nation to ratify the 18th Amendment.

Lesson 3

Answers will vary. It is important that reformers stay true to their hearts. Rarely do we have one and only one cause to support. Most of us support multiple causes.

Lesson 4

The Prohibition era of the 1920s prospered the Mafia and other organized crime syndicates in the United States. Federal efforts to enforce prohibition, including raids on speakeasies, were countered by well-organized bootlegging operations with national and international connections. These were multi-million dollar operations. Bootlegging liquor across the border from Canada was relatively easy and highly profitable.

Lesson 5

With all the sophisticated equipment and law enforcement capabilities, it is impossible for criminals to be so blatant in their criminal behavior.

Chapter 8

Lesson 1

Almost from the beginning public education was in trouble. It tried to teach students with individual goals by professionals in large groups of kids. This is impossible. Also, funding was a problem. It was the most expensive way to educate children.

Lesson 2

Answers will vary.

Lesson 3

Mann championed what many call "government schools" and when education was taken out of the home and the Church. It did not bode well for the future.

Lesson 4

An education is one of the few things that we can give ourselves and our children that will have lifelong effects. Although most American families send their children—as they themselves were sent by their own parents—to public schools, how often have we stopped to question the goals of the public education system? Christian parents especially should be asking this question if they are truly concerned whether their goals for educating their children are similar to the public schools'. Proverbs 1:7 tells us "the fear of the Lord is the beginning of knowledge." It should stand to reason that if "the fear of the Lord" is the beginning of knowledge, starting a quest for knowledge anywhere else will not yield true knowledge.

Lesson 5

With all the sophisticated equipment and law enforcement capabilities, it is impossible for criminals to be so blatant in their criminal behavior.

Chapter 9

Lesson 1

The first influence that brought evangelicalism, was the Anglican Church (the Church of England) and its emphasis on the small group, accountability meeting. These reforming societies were sponsored and defended quite strongly by John Wesley's father. Later, John and Charles Wesley formed the Methodist societies that held its members accountable to a strict ethical standard. Next, evangelicalism emerged from Calvinistic Protestantism in the Puritan movement. This was a movement that broke with Anglicanism on questions of church order, and emphasized the sovereignty of God in salvation, the comprehension of Christian assurance through the work of the Holy Spirit. The most notable proponent of this component of evangelicalism was Jonathan Edwards in America and George Whitefield in England. The final distinctive of evangelicalism emerged from European pietism. The European pietists pioneered lay preaching, youth ministry, an innovative hymnology, and an emphasis on privatistic and corporate prayer. The Moravians were the most famous evangelicals of this type.

Lesson 2

Evangelical movements expanded in Britain, but much more slowly and always in a complex connection with the Church of England. Evangelicalism remained intimately tied to the Church of England. It would be the same thing with the Church of Scotland—very strong evangelical elements, but Scotland was still the place dominated by the Church of Scotland—part of which was evangelical. In England and Scotland, evangelicalism formed no new denominations but remained in the traditional Protestant churches of both countries. In Great Britain evangelicalism was more of a reform movement; in America it was a whole new church expression or denomination.

Lesson 3

Answers will vary.

Lesson 4

"The scandal of the evangelical mind," he laments, "is that there is not much of an evangelical mind." Since the movement's birth in the transatlantic revivals of the early eighteenth century, it has brought millions to deep and lasting Christian faith. Even today, polls tell us, a solid majority of the folk who regularly attend and participate in the life of local churches are evangelical in belief and behavior. But in the process, Noll argues, they have paid a terrible price, for they have "abandoned the universities, the arts, and other realms of 'high' culture. The author agrees!

Lesson 5

Answers will vary.

Chapter 10

Lesson 1

The Scopes Trial, then, was a pivotal cultural battleground during the 1920s. The roots of this religious conflict were planted in the late 19th century. Before the Civil War, the Protestant denominations were united in a belief that the findings of science confirmed the teachings of religion. But during the 1870s, a lasting division had occurred in American Protestantism over Charles Darwin's theory of evolution. Religious modernists argued that religion had to be accommodated to the teachings of science, while religious traditionalists sought to preserve the basic tenets of their religious faith. During that trial, for the first time, America took stock of itself and rejected the Word of God.

Lesson 2

I would have insisted on arguing a constitutional case, period. I would have not allowed this case to be a referendum on the veracity of Scripture. No one at that trial was qualified to do that. Only Scripture can be used to judge Scripture—even the U. S. Constitution is an inferior document to the inspired, inerrant Word of God! Finally, I certainly would not have allowed

Darrow to cross examine me on the stand on national radio!

Lesson 3

Mr. Ham says, "If we allow our children to doubt the days of creation, when the language speaks so plainly, they are likely to then doubt Christ's Virgin Birth, and that He really rose from the dead."

Lesson 4

There are many from whom to choose. My favorite is Billy Graham whose humble faithfulness brought thousands into the Kingdom.

Lesson 5

Evangelicals, we are experiencing a cultural revolution, a violent one. We must not merely talk the talk, he must walk the walk. We must create an alternative community of hope. We must sabotage the conspiracy of hopelessness and self-centeredness that is so pervasive in our nation. Bring on the revolution!

Chapter 11

Lesson 1

The problem is, Germans did not know how to do this "democratic thing." Those who wanted, couldn't, because most Germans did not prefer this type of government. Bismarck successfully protracted his German alliance between Bavaria, Prussia, Hanover, et al., during the rise of the German Empire (1871-1914) through extending significant privileges to the middle class. Empowering and enriching the middle class—average working-class people—is the preferred way to build a new government. The thing is, though, like the French middle class in the rise of absolutism in France in the 18th century, the German middle class was willing to sacrifice democracy for the security that an oligarchy brought. They would do it in a heartbeat. Adolf Hitler had over 80% of the German vote in 1932 when he took over. He did not bully his way into Germany. He was invited in by the middle class! The German middle class, since the Nationalist movements of the post Napoleonic Europe, sought unification, a feat almost impossible, unless under a strong leadership, which Bismarck finally provided. This early era of German unification created a lot of the precedents that were to follow, of anti-democratic feeling, and the masses longing for strong leadership to see them through hard times. When push came to shove in the 1920s, when communism was a threat, when the economy collapsed, Germans were ready to abandon the Weimar Republic and democracy in a heartbeat. Strong tertiary leadership had worked for their grandparents, why not for them?

Lesson 2

The Weimar government participated in a delusion. Because it did not have sufficient tax revenue, because the economy was in a severe recession, it borrowed money to pay reparations. This created a vicious, downward cycle until Adolf Hitler took power.

Lesson 3

By 1930 the inflation had radically redistributed the wealth of Germany. The segment of society that was hit the hardest seems to have been the middle class. The poor had little wealth to lose while the rich were often able to get their wealth into forms not adversely affected by inflation. The middle class, to say the least, was ready for a change!

Lesson 4

The cabaret with its alternately unbridled euphoria and darkest despair is perhaps the best metaphor for the Weimar Republic. It invited both intelligent conversation and the severe reflection in an era that admittedly, with gross inflation, and economic chaos, to be surreal.

The cabarets became debate societies. It is not coincidence that Adolf Hitler began his rebellion in a 1920s Beer Hall! People could go to a cabaret, have a beer, some laughs and critique the state without the feeling that they were being disloyal. It was this transformation in public opinion that allowed cabaret to go from existing only in a technical sense in World War I to the powerful cultural, intellectual and political force it became in the Weimar Republic. To a large degree, the Nazi party was launched in cabarets.

Lesson 5

Given our heritage, it seems likely that we would not embrace totalitarianism or absolutism . . . but who knows. In crisis moments in the past—the American Civil War, 9-11, for instance—our democracy has worked. Why wouldn't it work in the face of even worse catastrophes?

Chapter 12

Lesson 1

The New Dealers were strongly influenced by the Progressive reformers of the early 20th century, who believed that government had not only a right but a duty to intervene in all aspects of economic life in order to improve the quality of American life. They, in effect, created the positive liberal state. In one significant respect, however, the New Dealers differed decisively from the Progressives. Progressive reform had a strong moral dimension; many reformers wanted to curb drinking, eliminate what they considered immoral behavior, and ameliorate human character. In comparison, the New Dealers were much more pragmatic. They sought to establish social policy without any connection to Judeo-Christian morality. Historian Steve Mintz states, "The New Deal did not end the Depression. Nor did it significantly redistribute income. It did, however, provide Americans with economic security that they had never known before. The New Deal legacies include unemployment insurance, old age insurance, and insured bank deposits. The Wagner Act reduced violence in labor relations. The Securities and Exchange Commission protected stock market investments of millions of small investors. The Federal Housing Administration and Fannie Mae enabled a majority of Americans to become homeowners. The New Deal's greatest legacy was a shift in government philosophy. As a result of the New Deal, Americans came to believe that the federal government has a responsibility to ensure the health of the nation's economy and the welfare of its citizens. This was an ominous development."

Lesson 2

"Hand in hand with this we must frankly recognize the overbalance of population in our industrial centers and, by engaging on a national scale in a redistribution, endeavor to provide a better use of the land for those best fitted for the land. The task can be helped by definite efforts to raise the values of agricultural products and with this the power to purchase the output of our cities. It can be helped by preventing realistically the tragedy of the growing loss through foreclosure of our small homes and our farms. It can be helped by insistence that the Federal, state, and local governments act forthwith on the demand that their cost be drastically reduced. It can be helped by the unifying of relief activities which today are often scattered, uneconomical, and unequal. It can be helped by national planning for and supervision of all forms of transportation and of communications and other utilities which have a definitely public character. There are many ways in which it can be helped, but it can never be helped merely by talking about it. We must act and act quickly."—President Roosevelt intends to use the government to redistribute wealth and influence.

Lesson 3

By 1930 the inflation had radically redistributed the wealth of Germany. The segment of society that was hit the hardest seems to have been the middle class. The poor had little wealth to lose while the rich were often able to get their wealth into forms not adversely affected by inflation. The middle class, to say the least was ready for a change!

Lesson 4

In spite of trillions of federal dollars being poured into social projects since the New Deal and War on Poverty in the middle sixties, there are more poor people today than any other time in American history. Even in the idealistic decade of 1960-70, when everyone thought the war on poverty would be won in a generation, in spite of the fact that the government provided unprecedented resources for children, the well-being of children declined.

Lesson 5

The wealthy, and the government, are consuming more resources than they are creating. They are therefore hurting the poor more than helping the poor.

Chapter 13

Lesson 1

Answers will vary. The story about Miss Sara is poignant. Also, the stories about the Yankees are interesting.

Lesson 2

In the midst of so much poverty and persecution the Church was a place of succor and affirmation.

Lesson 3

Assuming Mr. Calloway knew this fact, this was merely a raiding party and he must have known intuitively that they would not free him. Plus, they were pilfering his owner's food and this would have put everyone in a bad way.

Lesson 4

Answers will vary. What was it like to meet Mr. Lincoln? What did Robert E. Lee look like? John Brown?

Lesson 5

Chapter 14

Lesson 1

Answers will vary.

Lesson 2

It is conjecture but I suspect it did it to support his buddies. I don't think he was trying to be a hero or he had any great hatred toward the Germans.

Lesson 3

When someone is involved in something bigger than himself he wants to think it is very important. I am certain Mr. Manix was sincere, if not entirely accurate, in his assessment.

Lesson 4

A movie persuaded him to join the U. S. Marine Corps.

Lesson 5

Angry, discouraged, and disappointed.

Chapter 15

The Holocaust was the planned, systematic, bureaucratic, nation-sponsored murder of approximately six million Jews by the Nazi regime and its collaborators. The Jewish people were not the only victims. German authorities also targeted other groups because of their perceived "racial inferiority": Roma (Gypsies), the disabled, and some of the Slavic peoples (Poles, Russians, and others). Other groups were persecuted on political, ideological, and behavioral grounds, among them Communists, Socialists, Jehovah's Witnesses, Pentecostals, and homosexuals.

Lesson 2

The Magna Carta grants rights to individuals that are separate from, and not related to, the rights granted by the state. Likewise, American law, also based on the Magna Carta, but reinforced by the Bill of Rights, provides that human rights supersede judicial and legal rights. In other words, the state can take away my citizenship but all people "are endowed by their Creator with certain unalienable rights that among these are life, liberty, and the pursuit of happiness." These rights may be suspended in wartime—but only temporarily. These interventions cannot be codified into laws.

Lesson 3

This made the deportation of Jewish people to killing centers much easier.

Lesson 4

The Germans had to define, to gather, and to kill, and then dispose of, 10 million people. What could be more difficult? German ingenuity overcame these difficulties by passing the Nuremburg Laws, placing Jews in Ghettos, and then murdering them in killing centers.

Lesson 5

Merton wrote, "And so I ask myself: what is the meaning of a concept of sanity that excludes love, considers it irrelevant, and destroys our capacity to love other human beings, to respond to their needs and their sufferings, to recognize them also as persons, to apprehend their pain as one's own? Evidently this is not necessary for "sanity" at all. It is a religious notion, a spiritual notion, a Christian notion What business have we to equate "sanity" with "Christianity"? None at all, obviously. The worst error is to imagine that a Christian must try to be "sane" like everybody else, that we belong in our kind of society. That we must be "realistic" about it. We must develop a sane Christianity: and there have been plenty of sane Christians in the past." Eichmann separated his morality and faith from his "job."

Chapter 16

Lesson 1

Even before World War II ended, the Soviet Union had annexed much of Eastern Europe. There was another unsettling event. In August the nuclear age began and Russia had no nuclear weapons. In 1946, the Soviet Union rejected a U.S. proposal for an international agency to control nuclear energy production and research. The Soviets were convinced that the United States was trying to preserve its monopoly on nuclear weapons and it intended to have its own. In time it did, and an unnerving arms race began. A third source of conflict was post-war economic development assistance. While the United States generously rebuilt Western Europe with the Marshall Plan, the United States refused a Soviet request for massive reconstruction loans. In response, the Soviets called for substantial reparations from Germany and informally assumed an adversarial role with the United States.

Lesson 2

The conflict between the democratic west and the communist east was a geopolitical conflict. The difference between these two former friends was about land and security, two geopolitical considerations. Geopolitical issues concern the relationships that exist between a country's politics and its geography, or the influences that geography has on political relations between countries Russia wished to have a geographical buffer between itself and the West. For two times, one time very nearly fatally, Germany invaded Russia. She did not wish to see that happen again. The West, on the other hand, wished for each nation to decide for itself. The West knew that, given a choice, most nations would choose self-determination and democracy. There was also great resentment that Russia had replaced one tyranny with another. America had no geopolitical interest in Eastern Europe except as a buffer to Communist Russia! America had heard the Communist claim that a Communist revolution was inevitable and desirable in the whole world. So in a real way America and Russia wanted the same thing.

Lesson 3

The Korean War proved how difficult it was to achieve victory even under the best circumstances imaginable. In Korea, the United States faced a relatively weak adversary and had strong support from its allies. The United States possessed an almost total monopoly of sophisticated weaponry, yet the war dragged on for almost four years. Finally, the world had come to the brink of nuclear war and it was disorienting. The Korean War illustrated the difficulty of fighting a limited war. Limited wars are, by definition, fought for limited objectives. It is difficult to win a limited war but a nation dare not lose one. It is always unpopular because it is difficult to explain precisely what the country is fighting for and why the nation doesn't bomb the heck out of its opponents!   Finally, in Korea U.S. policymakers assumed that they could make the South Korean government do what they wanted. They involved themselves in nation building in a big way with mixed results. In reality, the situation was often reversed. The South Korean government really called the shots and America was unable to save face and withdraw from the war until it was unwinnable.

Lesson 4

Answers will vary. No doubt there would have been a worldwide thermo-nuclear war.

Lesson 5

America entered the war to stop the spread of communism. Technically speaking America did not lose the war. When America left in 1973 the South Vietnamese controlled their country. The South Vietnamese government could not build enough popular support for its government to counter successfully the North Vietnamese assault.

Chapter 17

Lesson 1

Movie theaters were the cathedrals of their age. Some seated 6500 and most Americans attended movie performances more often than churches. Cultural historians treat movies as sociological footprints that record the narrative and mood of particular historical settings; as cultural documents that present particular images of gender, ethnicity, and class.

Lesson 2

The first movies had no sound. Some film historians have argued that early silent films revolved around "characteristically working class settings," and expresse the interests of the poor in their struggles with the rich and powerful. In other words silent films dealt with motifs or themes popular in culture. Other scholars maintain that early movies drew largely upon conventions, stock characters, and routines derived from Wild West shows, comic strips, and other forms of late nineteenth-century popular entertainment. Charlie Chaplin, for instance, regularly played "stock" or "archetype characters."

Lesson 3

Talking movies dramatically changed the movie-going experience. Movie-goers were now expected to remain quiet. The movie theater, then, became a place of individual, private entertainment. While the community could share the same experience, it had to share it silently until later. No longer was the movie theater a social event where everyone shared their weekly events; it was a moment to reflect and to enjoy a world becoming increasingly distant from the world of most patrons.

Lesson 4

The Searchers, starring John Wayne, directed by John Ford, is, at its core, a movie about race (Levy, p. 1). While The Searchers in fact belongs in the western genre, "in its complexity and ambiguity, was a product of post-World War II American culture and sparked the deconstruction of the western film myth by looking unblinkingly at white racism and violence and suggesting its social psychological origins (Wayne State University Press)."

Lesson 5

The American love affair with technology will continue. One waits to see what will replace the Satosphere. The Satosphere is the quintessential Post-Modern entertainment. Individuals enter a theatre, are entertained, and experience unique experiences.

Chapter 18

Lesson 1

Rock 'n' roll traces its origins to the African-American slave community. Rock 'n' Roll began in the crucible f African culture, chattel slavery, and resulting slave resistance. Thus, from the beginning, rock 'n' roll was a subversive activity, a protest movement. In a sense, it never really lost that tone. Ironically, then, perhaps the only indigenous music of our free nation was from an enslaved society. Every society has its indigenous music, which serves as entertainment and accompaniment to ritual and ceremony. Our music was rock 'n' roll.

Lesson 2

There was a defiance, an anger in rock 'n' roll that protested the unjust treatment of African-Americans in American society. Rock 'n' roll was an inevitable outgrowth of the social and musical interactions between blacks and whites in the South. By mid 1930s, rock 'n' roll was everywhere. Elements of rock 'n' roll could be found in every type of American folk and blues music. By 1953, the phrase "rock 'n' roll" was used more widely to market the music beyond its initial African-American audience. When rock 'n' roll made a lot of money—through record sales and concerts—it became mainstream. Although some of the rhythm and blues musicians who had been successful in earlier years — such as Fats Domino who had his first hit in 1950 — were able to make the transition into new markets, markets that were appealing more and more to middle class whites. In fact much of the initial breakthrough into the wider pop music market came from white musicians, such as Elvis Presley and Jerry Lee Lewis. At the same time, younger black musicians such as Little Richard, Chuck Berry, and Bo Diddley become wildly popular and launched the rock 'n' roll era. By 1954 rock 'n' roll was the most popular music in America.

Lesson 3

It was no surprise to anyone that in the 1960s rock 'n' roll became increasingly reactionary and countercultural. As a matter of fact, rock music was the first American music genre to become socially relevant. The most important figure of the 1960s folk boom was Bob Dylan who invented the singer-songwriter, ballad genre. Inspired by people like Woody Guthrie and Pete Seeger, Dylan wrote deeply personal but relevant songs like "Blowin' in the Wind." There was a frenzy of new rock 'n' roll songs and groups to sing them. The Mommas and the Pappas, The Beatles, The Rolling Stones, The Grateful Dead, and The Beach Boys stormed American cultural walls.

Lesson 4

Answers will vary.

Lesson 5

"I was very proud back then," Barwick said. "I really thought one person could make a difference. We did make a difference, but not the difference we thought we could." While I do not think Woodstock was a good thing at all, it showed the idealism and hope that was so much a part of my generation. So much idealism has disappeared! No more dreams! It is sad.

Chapter 19

Lesson 1

Answers will vary.

Lesson 2

Technology helped make the 20th century the bloodiest in history. World War I, which introduced the machine gun, the tank, and poison gas, killed 10 million (almost all were soldiers). World War II, with its firebombs and nuclear weapons, produced 35 million war deaths. The Cold War added another 17 million deaths to the total. Technology made mass killing efficient; ideologies and ethnicity justified it. Underdeveloped countries driven to modernize quickly were often scenes of repression and sickening mass killing, whether they were communist or non-communist. Steven Mintz (http: www.digitalhistory.uh.edu/), Erich Goldhagen (Harvard Divinity School), Kermit Hall (Vanderbilt University).

Lesson 3

As a means of coping with these contrasting aspects of adolescence, youth create independence through behavior—specifically, through the leisure-oriented activities with peers. The steady and helpful hand of adults is lost in the shuffle, and significant enculturation deficiencies inevitably emerge.

Lesson 4

We don't like to work. Nobody wants to sacrifice. We're uninformed. I-culture.

Lesson 5

Certainly life is better in many wasys. We live longer. We live better. Yet, in many ways, things have not improved. Divorces have increased. Murder has increased. Poverty has increased.

Chapter 20

Lesson 1

In spite of gaining job skills and leverage in World War II, a growing numbers of women rejected higher education or a full-time career and, instead, preferred to be wives and mothers. In many ways, the social gains women gained in the 1940s were willingly abandoned in the 1950s and 1960s.

Lesson 2

The notion that Americans cannot choose their own light bulbs seems absurd!

A federal law bans most incandescent light bulbs, the familiar pear-shaped ones that almost all of us use in our homes. This was to preserve energy. Conventional 100 watt incandescent bulbs no longer were manufactured after January 1, 2012, while 75, 60, and 40 watt incandescent phased out over the following two years. Americans do not need this kind of "big brother"!

Lesson 3

The northern, white-dominated city has not been kind to African-Americans. This fact was not lost on their children — the generation who marched in Selma and burned the Watts section of Los Angeles. They formed the black nationalist movement — characterized by an emphasis on separatism and cultural exclusivity. What black Americans learned again was that resistance — not paternalism, not accommodation, not compromise — worked in American society. Ralph Ellison's grandfather on his death bed admonished young Ralph: ". . . our life is a war . . . we are spies in the enemy's camp . . . learn it to the younguns." By the middle 1960s, black nationalism, a primarily urban phenomenon, had captured much of the African-American agenda. In fact, black nationalism —a celebration of African-American culture as a separate entity — remains a powerful force in American culture.

Lesson 4

Shelby Steele write, "What is white guilt? It is not a personal sense of remorse over past wrongs. White guilt is literally a vacuum of moral authority in matters of race, equality, and opportunity that comes from the association of mere white skin with America's historical racism. It is the stigmatization of whites and, more importantly, American institutions with the sin of racism. Under this stigma white individuals and American institutions must perpetually prove a negative--that they are not racist--to gain enough authority to function in matters of race, equality, and opportunity. If they fail to prove the negative, they will be seen as racists. Political correctness, diversity policies, and multiculturalism are forms of deference that give whites and institutions a way to prove the negative and win reprieve from the racist stigma." Shelby Steele, "The age of white guilt: and the disappearance of the black individual," in *Harper's Magazine*, November 30, 1999.

Lesson 5

Saturday-morning television presented more orthodox, 1940-type heroes. In society at large, heroes were no longer paradigms of virtue; they were sensitive Freudian freaks who attracted more sympathy than admiration.

Chapter 21

Lesson 1

In most Western societies, there is a clear distinction between a government and the state. Public disapproval of a particular government (expressed, for example, by not re-electing an incumbent) does not necessarily represent disapproval of the state itself (i.e., of the particular framework of government). When Americans removed Jimmy Carter from office, they did not necessarily reject the American government or state. Often the state is sustained by a written constitution or common law. However, in some totalitarian regimes, there is not a clear distinction between the regime and the state.

Lesson 2

China is an oligarchy ruled by a small group of autocrats. Russia is in theory a democracy. The United States is a constitutional republic. The Vatican is a theocracy. England is a constitutional monarchy. France is a Republic.

Lesson 3

C

Lesson 4

By refusing to fund the war.

Lesson 5

It is unconstitutional for a public institution to discriminate against an American citizen because of race, gender, or national origin.

Chapter 22

Lesson 1

Answers will vary. America had the technology and resources to defeat the Russians. They also gained a technological edge by obtaining German scientists!

Lesson 2

While the author recognizes, indeed, lived through the Cold War crisis, no present need can justify the neglect of justice that our government so blatantly manifested in the name of exigency.

Lesson 3

Answers will vary.

Lesson 4

Among the problems that would need to be solved before a human trip to Mars could take place would be: It's a two-year round trip to Mars by a direct minimum energy orbit each direction, with a few months' wait at Mars as well. The current world record for the longest duration in space is about half that time and there are serious medical problems the Russian cosmonauts have encountered when they return to Earth. Next, to send people to Mars, the mission will need to take everything it needs to get there, and live in space for two years. A direct approach like that used for the Apollo missions to get to the moon (take everything needed and throw it away in pieces as it gets used up) won't work for Mars: the mass required to get to Mars and back is well beyond the capability of even the most powerful rockets ever made. What's it going to be like there? Before putting astronauts on Mars, NASA needs to explore Mars in great detail

Lesson 5

Extraterrestrial life is defined as life that does not originate from earth. Possible forms of extraterrestrial life range from simple bacteria-like organisms to human creatures. Various claims have been made for evidence of extraterrestrial life. According to this argument, endorsed by scientists such as Carl Sagan and Stephen Hawking, it would be improbable for life not to exist somewhere other than Earth. However, the author believes this to be untrue—God created life and there is no evidence in Scripture that He created it anywhere but on earth.

Chapter 23

Lesson 1

Divorce has doubled. Couples are cohabiting before marriage at an alarming rate. The majority of American children grow up in single families or in blended families. All these problems—and they are problems—are interconnected.

Lesson 2

Blankenhorn's insightful analysis of the state of American fathers in modern America is disarmingly simple: the Unnecessary Father (Ch. 4), the Old Father (Ch. 5), the New Father (Ch. 6), the Deadbeat Dad (Ch. 7), the Visiting Father (Ch. 8), the Sperm Father (Ch. 9), the Stepfather and the Nearby Guy (10), and, our hero, the Good Family Man (Ch. 11). One of the reasons this book is destined to influence social welfare policy as well as social mores is that its structure is so inescapably simple and right. The Unnecessary Father (typical notion that dads are not necessary), the Old Father (the macho, mean, domineering father), and the New Father (the sensitive, liberated, androgyny dad) are the most common garden variety dads we will meet in our society today. The other five roles are minor but insightful. The Deadbeat Dad is the bad guy, the guy who does not pay child support. The Visiting Father is a victim, a pathetic example of what fathering has become, proof positive that fathers are not important after all. The Stepfather and the Nearby Guy are surrogate dads, magnanimously assuming the role of father of father for Deadbeat dads/jerks who have abandoned their kids. Again, though, the Nearby Guy/Stepfather is a rather innocuous version of what fathers should be. Blankenhorn uses the example of the Disney movie *The Incredible Journey* (1993) where a poor example of a father slowly earns the right to be a dad by sheepishly giving into his stepchildren's wants.

Lesson 3

Conservatives seek to deny or to restrict access to abortion, restrict explicit sexual content on television, and limit teenagers' access to contraceptive information. Liberals are more willing to use government social policies to strengthen family life. Some of the proposals they have made to strengthen families include expanded nutritional and health programs for pregnant women, federal subsidies for day care services for low-income families, uniform national standards for child care centers, and a requirement that employers give parents unpaid leave to take care of a newborn or seriously ill child. Most social liberals are reticent to deal with moral, ethical issues, since, in their mind, these are private, not public, concerns.

Lesson 4

In conclusion, Galatians 3:28 is speaking of the accessibility of salvation to all people without regard to gender. It is not discussing role distinctions in the home or in the church, so other passages that define limitations in roles because of gender are not to be disregarded. While limitations undoubtedly were given in response to a specific problem situation, as the occasion demanded, there is no need to consider the limiting passages as contradictions of a general rule found in Galatians 3:28. Since Paul is the author of all of them, there is no reason to conclude that he saw a contradiction or that 1 Corinthians 14:33-35 and 1 Timothy 2:1-15 were temporary exceptions based on mitigating circumstances. There is no reason for us not to interpret all three passages as a harmonious whole. Therefore, Galatians 3:28 does not overrule Paul's instruction in 1 Corinthians 14:33-35 or 1 Timothy 2:1-15.

Lesson 5

A. 'What is it--what?' she said.—The grieving mom is not sure what death is and how it took her baby.

B. I thought, Who is that man? I didn't know you.—The mom's grief has come between her and her husband.

C. 'You--oh, you think the talk is all. I must go-- Somewhere out of this house. How can I make you--'— The mom is alienated form her husband forced to leave the one who loves her. Her Naturalistic views of life alientate and discurage her.

Chapter 24

Lesson 1

While we are rediscovering the city's mission field and introducing an urban methodology, our biblical and theological reflection is limited. We enter the city equipped with an urban sociology and urban tools for ministry, but we carry with us the baggage of a theology designed in rural Europe. Even the very way we formulate theological questions and the frameworks we use to construct our theological thought have been forged from our rural past. What we are in need of is a theology as urban as our sociology and missiology—a theology, as Ray Bakke puts it, "as big as the city itself"! (Robert Linthicum)

Lesson 2

Supply cannot keep up with demand in densely populated areas. Until comparatively recently, people lived in village communities and their culture, mode of living, food and social organization were adjusted to their surroundings. Modern urbanized life has produced a new environment, creating new problems of adaptation. It is one thing for 4000 people in the steppes of Mongolia to adjust to their new surroundings; it is quite another for 15 million people to do the same thing in Mexico City.

Lesson 3

The city is in trouble. Cities all over America are approaching fiscal insolvency. Even in the midst of wealth, cities are failing. In 1990, for instance, the city of Bridgeport, located in Connecticut's wealthiest county, became the nation's first major city to file for bankruptcy. American cities are bled dry and abandoned by suburbia and the federal government an I doubt the situation will improve in the next twenty years.

Lesson 4

Theologian Walter Brueggemann calls "history makers. Brueggemann explains that history is not necessarily made by people with lots of money, prestige, or even education. Our study of race relations tells us that history is made by anyone — especially the Church — who is willing to be obedient to God at all costs. Jeremiah was a history maker, Brueggemann explains. In spite of being part of an oppressed, defeated people, Jeremiah understood that history is made by a people of God — rich, poor, weak, or powerful. Jeremiah understood that God makes history; that God is in control of Babylon, Moscow, Washington D.C., and Johnstown. That God determines the future — no matter what circumstances may imply. And Jeremiah's circumstances were pretty bleak. It is 588 B.C. and Judah is one year away from total destruction at the hands of the Babylonians. The inept King Zedekiah has imprisoned Jeremiah. But worse still, Jeremiah knows full well that the future only holds defeat and heartache As the Jewish theologian Abraham Heschel describes Jeremiah, "The Word of the Lord is upon me and I was so alone." In 29:4-9 Jeremiah warns his nation that they must settle down in Babylon and get used to exile. The displacement is real and serious and will last. They are to entertain no wishful thinking about its quick end and a "return to normalcy." But invest in the dream, bu the land that you may never live to enjoy — the field at Anatoth — because you believe in the dream. And some day, Jeremiah insists, God will bring us home. "I will restore your fortunes and gather you from all the nations and all the places where I have driven you . . . and I will bring you back to the place from which I sen you into exile!" Brueggemann warns us that a history maker is committed to reality. Jeremiah knew that the future is bleak — and we also know that there is still much work to be done. But Jeremiah believed in God's ultimate triumph.

Lesson 5

Answers will vary.

Chapter 25

Lesson 1

There is no doctrine, no objective corpus of truth. Ther are only stories. Everyone wants to tell his/her "story." It does not matter what our theology is — what matters s that we tell our stories and listen sympathetically to other stories. There is no objective truth from which to work. Post-Modern churches do therapy — no real ministry can occur.

Lesson 2

To Post-Modern architects there is no "pure" form or "perfect" architectonic detail. Post-Modernism draws from all architectural motifs (Victorian, Georgian, Modern, et al.) and in the process creates created a new architectural form altogether.

Lesson 3

To the Post-Modern, however, the Post-Modern sublime occurs when we are affected by a multitude of unpresentables without reference to reason as their unifying origin. Justice, then, cannot be definable but it is the ability to move and to judge among realities in their heterogeneity and multiplicity. Post-Moderns and Kant, of course, both have it wrong. Justice is acting in a fashion that is in line with the Will of God. Beauty is anything that manifests the manifestly immutable character of our most beautiful, awesome God whose Word is immutable, objective, inerrant, and inspired. Take that Mr. Kant!

Lesson 4

The central motif that Post-Modern America must understand is the cross. Paul had no trouble defining his gospel and his life as "the message of the cross." On the contrary, he boldly declared that, though the cross seemed either foolishness or a stumbling block to the self-confident (i.e., Modern humankind!) it was in fact the very essence of God's wisdom and power (1 Cor. 1:18-25). I yearn, as Dietrich Bonhoeffer did at the end of his life, for the crucified Lord to return again — as the rediscovered center — to the center of the Church and American society. The world does not need a new religion — it needs Jesus Christ — crucified and resurrected. Don't get me wrong. What I am suggesting is truly revolutionary, or, as Walter Brueggemann suggests "subversive." The church — my church — must be called to a higher commitment. A radical commitment. The choice for Christ occupies first place, above parents, children, job, and, if necessary, life itself. The gate leading to health and wholeness in our world is not reasonable size. It is narrow. In that sense, I am calling us all to a radical faith, a prophetic faith. We are called to a major reclamation project of our views of atonement so completely presented in Scripture and in our Confessions. Oh how my heart yearns for revival! For our world to reclaim the centrality of the cross! With John Stott, in *The Cross of Christ*, my prayer

is that this new generation, haunted by so many bad memories, so bewitched by technology and social science theories, would again come to the cross of our Lord Jesus Christ. And, at the same time, I want us to reclaim the joy of this adventure — so persuasively presented by John Piper in *Desiring God*. That we would no longer settle for the mud pies of delight our world offers us but, like the Puritans, would reclaim the delights of a life centered on the Lordship of Jesus Christ! That we would again enjoy the Lord — which is after all what worship and praise is.

Lesson 5

Os Guinness warns us that at some point Americans will become fed up with the excesses and dysfunctional aspects of our culture. He says that as American mainline culture fails to sustain Americans in their hedonistic pursuit of self interest, they will want something more. William Bennett is right to warn us that there is a "death of outrage" in our country but he might add that there is a numbness spreading across the land that offers much opportunity for Christians in general and for homeschoolers in particular. Guinness encourages Christians with the fact that Americans in the near future will be looking to places of stability and strength for direction. Besides, almost by default, those people whose lives are in reasonable good shape, who have some reason to live beyond the next paycheck will have almost an inexorably appeal. Like Aeneas in Virgil's *Aeneid* we will all someday after the storm thrown on somebody's beach. In summary, quite literally this generation will have to create a new world. How to create a new society? These are the new Pilgrims, the new Puritans. In Joseph Conrad's *Lord Jim*, Jim is instructing a young person steering a ship how to handle a storm. "Steer neither to the right or to the left of it," Lord Jim says, "Steer right into it." Christian homeschoolers, we need to steer right into the storm. We can be and will be more than conquerors in Christ Jesus!

Chapter 26

Lesson 1

Answers will vary. The author's family would fall in an eclectic category, with a mixture of middle states and southern food.

Lesson 2

Colson argues, "Don't forget: If we go against the way God designed us to live, it is like cutting across the grain of the universe, and we're asking for trouble. All we have to do to live right is to get with the plan—His plan, that is."

Lesson 3

Answers will vary.

Lesson 4

There are many theories about why the Recession occurred. Concerning the United States economy, proponents of free-market capitalism declare that Federal Reserve Chairman Ben Bernanke should not have bailed out failing firms and instead should have allowed free-market capitalism to quickly recover as it did in the depression of 1920 without government intervention (free-market capitalists assert that government intervention merely drags out recessions and depressions). A 2005 study found that government corporate bailouts are often done for mere political considerations and the economic resources allocated exhibit significantly worse economic performance than resources allocated using purely business considerations.

Lesson 5

The author states, "In our own country, at the beginning of the millennium, in spite of unprecedented prosperity, we see the seeds of our destruction everywhere. Increased crime, poverty, and unemployment. Hopelessness and domestic violence. Some of us wonder whether our American covenant is being recklessly compromised by some leaders who are choosing to condone practices that we see as immoral. We see Hazael. He will survive . . . but will we? Will the American dream survive." Before the end of the essay, however, the author is optimistic that in the days, weeks, and years ahead God will bring a great revival! He believes this because he knows that God is lifting up a whole new generation of faithful believers who are absolutely intrepid, smart, and godly.

Chapter 27

Lesson 1

While we place limits on ourselves, our God is illimitable in His possibilities for us if we are obedient!

Lesson 2

C. S. Lewis writes, "The contradiction "we must have faith to believe and must believe to have faith" belongs to the same class as those by which the Eleatic philosophers proved that all motion is impossible. And there are many others. You can't swim unless you can support yourself in water, and you can't support yourself

in water unless you can swim. Or again, in an act of volition (e.g., getting up in the morning) is the very beginning of the act itself voluntary or involuntary? If voluntary, then you must have willed it, . . . you were willing it already, . . . it was not really the beginning. If involuntary, then the continuation of the act (being determined by the first movement) is involuntary too. But in spite of this we do swim, and we do get out of bed."

Lesson 3

God does not want sacrifice; He wants obedience. So, if there is persecution, God is honoring His saints. It is up to us to see that, and to grasp its signficance to our faith

Lesson 4

Shaeffer writes, "Through the recent difficulties I have faced, the Lord taught me more than I ever knew of the greatness of the Lord and the smallness of any man -and the corresponding importance of pleasing the Lord, and the lack of importance of pleasing any particular man. . . . In spite of all that has happened there is no question of personal discouragement, for I am probably less discouraged than I have ever been since those bright days when I first saw the face of the Lord, and before my feet got stuck in the problems of the prestige of man. . . ."

Lesson 5

Those who give receive more than they give back. The Sisters of Mercy are about leading people into the Kingdom of God, not merely offering physical succor.

Chapter 28

Lesson 1

The university was started almost exclusively to train clergy.

Lesson 2

In fact, the American university was built solidly on evangelical principles. There were no so-called "official" "secular" colleges until the rise of the land grant college in the middle of the 19th century. An early brochure, published in 1643, stated that the purpose of Harvard University (the oldest American university) was "To advance Learning and perpetuate it to Posterity; dreading to leave an illiterate Ministry to the Churches. Harvard's motto for 300 years was "Christo et Ecclesiae. In fact, most of the U. S. universities founded before the 20th century had a strongly religious, usually Protestant Evangelical Christian character. Yale, Princeton, Chicago, Stanford, Duke, William and Mary, Boston

University, Michigan, and the University of California had a decidedly evangelical Christian character in the early years of their existence but abandoned it by the 20th century. By 1920s, the American university had stepped completely back from its evangelical roots. This was true of almost every American university founded in the first 200 years of our existence.

Lesson 3

Take responsibility for your life. Moses accepted responsibility for his life. "He chose to be mistreated along with the people of God rather to enjoy the pleasures of sin for a short time." (Hebs. 11: 25) If you don't make decisions for your life, someone else will. Get a cause worth dying for. Moses accepted necessary suffering even unto death. You need a cause worth dying for (as well as living for). "He [Moses] regarded disgrace for the sake of Christ as of greater value than the treasures of Egypt, because he was looking ahead to his reward." (Heb. 11: 26). We are crucified with Christ, yet it is not we who live but Christ who lives in us (Gal. 2:20). Finally, never take your eyes off the goal. "By faith, he left Egypt, not fearing the king's anger; he persevered because he saw Him who is invisible." (Heb. 11:27). What is your threshold of obedience?

Lesson 4

Central to Pelikan's thesis is an ongoing dialogue with John Henry Newman's The Idea of a University Defined and Illustrated (1852) (p. X). Newman's Idea of a University grew out of Newman's struggle with the rise of scientific learning — a struggle that continues today. Newman, it seems to me, is a 19th-century evangelical trying to come to grips with his culture. Pelikan is a twentieth century intellectual coming to grips with his Christianity. "A university," Newman wrote, "is not a birthplace of poets or of immortal authors, or founders of schools, leaders of colonies, or conquerors of nations. It does promise a generation of Aristotles or Newtons. . . a university training is the great ordinary means to a great but ordinary end; it aims at raising the intellectual tone of society . . ." In other words, the purpose of an education is to enable a person to live a life rather than to earn a living. Pelikan adds his own interpretation: The view taken of a university in these discourses is the following: that it is a place of teaching universal knowledge, but also of advancing knowledge through research and of diffusing knowledge through publication, as well as of relating such advancement, teaching, and diffusion to the training of professionals (p. 88).

Lesson 5

WHEREAS, through the good hand of God, many well devoted persons have been, and daily are moved, and stirred up, to give and bestow, sundry gifts, legacies, lands, and revenues for the advancement of all good literature, arts, and sciences in Harvard College, in Cambridge in the County of Middlesex, and to the maintenance of the President and Fellows, and for all accommodations of buildings, and all other necessary provisions, that may conduce to the education of the English and Indian youth of this country, in knowledge and godliness.

Chapter 29

Lesson 1
Answers will vary.

Lesson 2
Answers will vary.

Lesson 3
Answers will vary.

Lesson 4
Answers will vary.

Lesson 5
Answers will vary.

Chapter 30

Lesson 1
Europe is full of competitive, antagonistic people groups. Only in the last 50 years has there been a serious attempt to unify them.

Lesson 2
The differences are profound and substantial. America was formed from 13 states that had a similar heritage and religious background. The comparison of the two political entities is spurious.

Lesson 3
Sociologists explain that America and Europe approach work differently. Edward Crane and David Boaz, in what is now a fairly dated understanding of European politics, *An American vision: policies for the '90s,* explained how America embraced the Protestant work ethic (especially the English version) with enthusiasm. For an American, time is money. For a European, time is something one enjoys.

Lesson 4

Answers will vary.

Lesson 5

Rifkin argues, "The point, however, is not whether the Europeans are living up to their dream. We Americans have never fully lived up to our own dream. What's important is that a new generation of Europeans is creating a radical new vision for the future — one better suited to meet the challenges of an increasingly globalizing world in the 21st century." Such an unsubstantiated assumption is both radical and uninformed. Rifkin, like so many New Left historians, replace solid scholarsip with self-rigteous naval gazing.

Chapter 31

Lesson 1

The truth is, the Manchu Chinese never saw themselves as equal with anyone, much less the uncouth European traders who sought to do commerce with the great China. This sort of haughtiness remains in China even today. How ironical that English trader, in particular, saw themselves as superior to the yellow, slant-eyed Chinese who saw themselves superior to the pallid, wrinkled Westerners! One historian explained, "It wasn't that they rejected the idea of a community of nations; it's that they couldn't conceive of it. It would be like trying to teach a Buddhist monk about the Father, Son, and the Holy Ghost. This viewpoint was so pervasive that Chinese reformers who advocated more flexibility in China's dealings with the West were often accused of being Westerners with Chinese faces."

Lesson 2

That is a knotty question. Winston Churchill said he would support Satan himself to defeat Adolf Hitler— and so England supported Communist Russia. It seems to me, however, that that was shortsighted. England should not have supported Russia, and the USA was right in not supporting the Communists (Stilwell's request was denied).

Lesson 3

Often, but not always, nationalist revolutions are based on the notion that people are bacically good and only need to be released from repressive regimes and there will be a Utopia. However, such a notion is wrong. Eventually, revolutions based on mankind's "goodness" evolve into totalitarian nightmares.

Lesson 4

An educated young Christian described her church to me: "We have 50 young professionals in this church. Everyone is so busy working, you don't have time for socializing, and even if you are socializing, you are putting on a fake face. But in church people feel warm, they feel welcome… they feel people really love them so they really want to join the community, a lot of people come for this."

Lesson 5

It is unlikely that a Communist country of any type will supplant a free capitalist country of American economic power.

Chapter 32

Lesson 1

In the 19th century and early 20th century most terrorism was tied to Nationalism. These devotees were driven by the interests or culture of a group of people or a nation. A Serbian nationalist murdered the crown prince of the Austro-Hungarian Empire. Typically, nationalists share a common ethnic background and wish to establish or regain a homeland. In the 21st century most terrorism is connected to religion. Religious extremists often reject the authority of secular governments and view legal systems that are not based on their religious beliefs as illegitimate. They often view modernization efforts as corrupting influences on traditional culture.

Lesson 2

Terrorism, whatever its initial genesis entailed, eventually emerged as a violent, disruptive, anarchist movement whose ideology was secondary to its praxis, or even absent altogether.

Lesson 3

During the immediate postwar period, terrorism was more of a tactical choice by leaders of nationalist insurgencies and revolutions. Successful campaigns for independence from colonial rule occurred throughout the world, and many employed terrorism as a tactic. Again, it worked nicely. A relatively small group of dedicated fanatics could affect the policy of powerful nations. The feeling was euphoric and addictive. Run a stupid speed boat full of explosives into the side of an American warship and one made the evening news, an even better, could drive the greatest nation on the face of the Earth to remove its troops from Somalia! When terrorism was used, it was used within the framework of larger movements, and coordinated with political, ocial, and military action. Even when terrorism came o dominate the other aspects of a nationalist struggle, uch as the Palestinian campaign against Israel, it ngendered, and fed off, ancillary causes. Large nation tates made terrorism much easier by providing huge mounts of money and weaponry to make terrorism nore effective. During the Cold War, the Soviet Union rovided direct and indirect assistance to revolutionary novements around the world. Of course supporting errorism is like holding a rattle snake—it bites the ne holding the snake as well as the person next to the erson holding the snake. Russia was itself attacked by Chechen terrorists.

Lesson 4

Answers will vary. Certainly this illegal organization nvolved itself in some excesses, however, never did t commit the acts of random violence, which are the alling card of contemporary terrorism.

Lesson 5

No. The War on Terrorism has only begun. Nowhere is t over or much less won.

Chapter 33

Lesson 1

A pandemic is an epidemic of infectious disease that is preading through human populations across a large egion or even worldwide. A widespread endemic lisease that is stable in terms of how many people are getting sick from it is not a pandemic. It is conceivable hat a pandemic could destroy the human population of the world. AIDS, as awful as it is, is not a pandemic. AIDS is isolated to one particular group and is mostly promulgated by this group's behavior.

Lesson 2

Answers will vary. The author suggests that the evidence s inconclusive.

Lesson 3

agree that the threat of a biological or nuclear attack is eal.

Lesson 4

Fears of over population have been excuses for nfanticide and abortion.

Lesson 5

Answers will vary.

Chapter 34

Lesson 1
With such a talented pool of young people entering the leadership of this country I am optimistic that Scenario 1 is most plausaible.

Lesson 2
I wholeheartedly agree and am concerned that the media has become the message (by Neil Postman).

Lesson 3
Thankfully not yet, but it appears that we might be heading that way.

Lesson 4
Answers will vary.

Lesson 5
Answers will vary.

◄● Exam Answer Keys

Chapter 1 Exam Options

Option 1 – Matching:

1. Pragmatism: Philosophical view that argues for ordinary, common sense.
2. Epistemology: The study of knowledge.
3. Avant-Garde: Forward thinking, modern.
4. Surrealism: Out of the real of ordinary experience.
5. Moral Relativism: Morality based on circumstances.

Option 2 – Essay:

The emerging generation would indeed make policy for most of the world in the next 20-40 years. The problem was that most of my classmates were not following the Word of God. They were not committed to advancing the Kingdom of God as much as they were committed to advancing their own agendas. The world, I must say, has entered a post-Christian era, partly because of my classmates sitting in that chapel in 1976.

Chapter 2 Exam Options

Option 1 – Matching:

1. Margaret Sanger: A racist advocate of birth control.
2. "One Big Union for All": Was the goal of the radical labor leaders and Socialists who met in Chicago in 1905.
3. Social Gospel: A theory of helping the needy and poor based on human good, not the Bible.
4. Theodore Roosevelt: Great progressive president.
5. Rough Riders: Roosevelt's Spanish American troops who took San Juan Hill.

Option 2 – Essay:

Muckraking reporters, exploiting mass circulation journalism, attacked malfeasance in American politics and business. They embraced lost, obscure causes, championed aberrant positions, created conflict and confusion, all in order to increase circulation. President Theodore Roosevelt gave them the name "muckrakers" after a character in the book *Pilgrim's Progress*, "the Man with the Muckrake," who was more preoccupied with filth than with Heaven above. They did some good. Popular magazines such as *McClure's*, *Everybody's*, *Pearson's*, *Cosmopolitan*, and *Collier's* published articles exposing the evils of American society — political corruption, stock market manipulation, fake advertising, vices, impure food

and drugs, racial discrimination, and lynching. Upton Sinclair's *The Jungle* exposed unsanitary conditions in the meat-packing industry. But a dangerous precedent was set: the media, immune to the electorate, or any other controls, was committed to sensationalism over truth, if it increased circulation. The media for the first time felt no obligation to embrace any standard but its own (a Modernist tendency). Furthermore, it accepted no policy that would force it to show any objectivity whatsoever. The media abandoned all facade of altruism and fairness, and became a parochial, chauvinistic profit-making machine, answerable to no one.

Chapter 3 Exam Options

Option 1 – Matching:

1. Kulturkampf: Stuggles in culture.
2. Dreadnoughts: Large battleships thought to be unsinkable.
3. The Socialist Party: Represented the middle class; became important in the German Empire.
4. Militarism: National philosophy of military power.
5. A constitutional monarchy: In effect a democracy, and in Britain's case it also had a huge empire.

Option 2 – Essay:

Technology and science separated from ethics and morality will bring horrible results. We see the same problem in World War II when Germany, the most advanced nation in the world, used technology and false science to murder 6 million people.

Chapter 4 Exam Options

Option 1 – Matching:

1. Oswald Bölcke: Joined the German Air Corps in 1914 and fought in every major engagement until he went missing in action in 1916.
2. Biplanes: Early airplanes with dual wings that helped them maneuver.
3. Field hospitals: Emergency medical centers set up out where the battles ensued.
4. Lt. Col. George Brenton Laurie: From Nova Scotia; appointed a special service officer, including the command of a mounted infantry battalion for the South African War.
5. Chaplain George T. McCarthy: Roman Catholic chaplain who made an effort to focus on the Lord in the midst of danger and death.

Option 2 – Essay:

War, any crisis, has a way of stripping away our façades and forcing us to look at our God squarely in the face. These poor souls believed in God, in friendships, and in their own fate, in that order. They were not embracing something as frigid and abstract as Modernism.

Chapter 5 Exam Options

Option 1 – Matching:

1. Vaudeville: A form of comedy entertainment.
2. Neurasthenia: National anxiety.
3. Morrill Act: Federal act to set up lend lease colleges.
4. Mass communication: Forms of media that reach a broad, national audience.
5. Yellow journalism: Sensational, salacious writings to persuade an audience to buy into a lie.

Option 2 – Essay:

Technology, if used properly, makes Americans more efficient and productive. It can therefore, give Americans more time to do better things—like spending time with family members and reading the Bible.

Chapter 6 Exam Options

Option 1 – Matching:

1. Crew of Battleship Potemkin: Russian participants in the 1905 Revolution.
2. Czar Nicholas II: Czar when the Russian Revolution arrived.
3. Duma: The Russian Parliament.
4. Lenin: Leader of the Russian Revolution.
5. Bolshevism: Russian Communism.

Option 2 – Essay:

From the beginning, communism had could not maintain egalitarian rule. The human heart needs the discipline and limits of government. Communism was a form of anarchy. Ultimately, the communists formed a totalitarian regime that would have made Adolf Hitler proud. Next, no state will be productive if it does onto reward ingenuity and entrepreneurial savvy and acumen and initiative.

Chapter 7 Exam Options

Option 1 – Matching:

1. 18th Amendment: Outlawed the sale of alcohol products in the U. S. A.
2. Nativist: A group who opposed immigration of all sorts.
3. Prohibition: Banning the production and sale of alcohol.
4. Volstead Act: Defined intoxicating beverages as anything with more than 0.5 percent alcohol.
5. The Woman's Christian Temperance Union (WCTU): Organized by women concerned about the destructive power of alcohol.

Option 2 – Essay:

There was too much money to be made in alcohol manufacture, distribution, and consumption. Speakeasies thrived because they were frequented. It is a sad testimony to the American character that they were.

Chapter 8 Exam Options

Option 1 – Matching:

1. Homeschooling: A movement that has existed through all of American history but has become more popular since the 1970s.
2. Horace Mann: Early leader in public education.
3. Raymond Moore: Pioneer in home education.
4. John Holt: Educator who was critical of orthodox education.
5. Unschooling: The educational philosophy of John Holt's followers; what he called "learning by living."

Option 2 – Essay:

Answers will vary. As American society comes under more stress, one would expect public education to become more and more dysfunctional.

Chapter 9 Exam Options

Option 1 – Matching:

1. Second Great Awakening: The great revival in American in the 19th century.
2. Harold Ockenga: A great evangelist who founded Fuller Seminary.
3. Crucicentrism: Cross-centered theology.
4. John Wesley: The founder of Methodism.
5. Jonathan Edwards: American philosopher and theologian.

Option 2 – Essay:

Answers will vary.

Chapter 10 Exam Options

Option 1 – Matching:

1. Butler Act: Tennessee law that made the teaching of evolution illegal.
2. American Civil Liberties Union: A private liberal organization devoted to upholding the Constitution.
3. Clarence Darrow: The successful lawyer at the Scopes Trial.
4. William Jennings Bryan: A great American statesman.
5. National Stumping: To hold informal mass rallies in support of a position or ideology.

Option 2 – Essay:

Answers will vary. Write a new history book, like Perry and Olasky, and let's hope that people read it! There is not much we can do to influence the liberal media, so, in the long run, we need to create our own media center and offer a more balanced, truthful story of world events.

Chapter 11 Exam Options

Option 1 – Matching:

1. Weimar Republic: A period of German democracy after WWI and before the Nazis took power.
2. German Reich: A German government.
3. Reparation: Money paid as punishment for the loss of a war.
4. Protective Tariffs: Duties placed on goods to protect indigenous industries.
5. McCarthy Era: A time of heightened fear against Communism in the U. S. A.

Option 2 – Essay:

This might have worked except with run-away inflation, and a severe recession, it is unlikely that the Weimar Republic would have survived under any conditions.

Chapter 12 Exam Options

Option 1 – Matching:

1. Great Depression: A time of great economic stress, 1929-1940.
2. The New Deal: Roosevelt's legislation intervention.
3. Positive Liberal State: A state with a lot of government intervention.
4. National Recovery Administration: A New Deal agency committed to oversight of labor and management.
5. Public Works Administration: Job creation agency in the New Deal.
6. Herb Block: A political cartoonist.

Option 2 – Essay:

Answers will vary. Offer tax incentives to big business so that it can expand and diversify. Offer generous business loans. In short, rebuild the nation by enabling the private sector to do so.

Chapter 13 Exam Options

Option 1 – Matching:

1. Federal Writers' Project (FWP): Sent writers into 1? states to interview ordinary people in order to write down their life stories.
2. John A. Lomax: National Advisor on Folklore and Folkways for the FWP.
3. Mary Reynolds: Born in slavery to the Kilpatrick family, she claimed to be more than a hundred years old.
4. Walter Calloway: Lived to be 89, with most of his life spent on the south side of Birmingham.
5. Ben Horry: From Murrells Inlet, South Carolina, and told his account of slavery.

Option 2 – Essay:

It is hard to tell. Generally they did not harm many slaves. Was that because they were humane? Or was it because slaves were property slave owners wished to keep their property healthy? Some slave-owners used overseers, independent contractors, to supervise their slaves and their farms. These generally were much crueler than the owners.

Chapter 14 Exam Options

Option 1 – Matching:

1. The Nuclear Age: A period that of nuclear power that gained prominence at the end of World War II.
2. Leona Cox: A Red Cross nurse during World War II.
3. Andrew Melendrez: Sergeant in the US Army fighting in Europe during World War II.
4. John William Manix: Fought with the US Army in the Pacific.
5. Carlisle Evans: Fought with the Marines in the Pacific.

Option 2 – Essay:

Oral history is the collection of historical information about individuals, important events, or everyday life using audiotapes, videotapes, or transcriptions of planned interviews. It is a time-honored way to gather historical information, but it obviously is only one perspective. However, collecting several different interviews will make the record more historically accurate.

Chapter 15 Exam Options

Option 1 – Matching:

1. Anti-Semitism: Systematic prejudice against Jewish people.
2. Holocaust: Murder of millions Jews during World War II.
3. National Socialist government: Nazi government.
4. Mischlinge: A German designation for a Jewish person.
5. Nuremberg Laws of 1935: Determined who was Jewish and who was not.
6. Gleichschaltung: Take over by Nazis of the civil services.
7. Einsatzgruppen: Mobile killing units in Russia.
8. Ghettoization: Placing Jews in containment areas for later deportation.
9. Final Solution: German plan to kill all the Jews in Europe.
10. Wannsee Conference: A German conference to deal with the extermination of the Jews.

Option 2 – Essay:

Between 1880 and the start of World War I in 1914, about two million Jews immigrated from Eastern Europe. Many settled clustered in New York City, created the garment industry there, which supplied the dry goods stores across the country, and were heavily engaged in the trade unions. Jewish immigration was curtailed with the birth of the Immigration Restriction League, and congressional studies by the Dillingham Commission from 1907 to 1911. The Emergency Quota Act of 1921 established immigration restrictions specifically on these groups, and the Immigration Act of 1924 further tightened and codified these limits. With the ensuing Great Depression, and despite worsening conditions for European Jews, with the rise of Nazi Germany, these quotas remained in place with minor alterations until the Immigration and Nationality Act of 1965.

Chapter 16 Exam Options

Option 1 – Matching:

1. Iron Curtain: A metaphor for the closing of the borders between free, democratic Europe and Soviet-controlled Eastern Europe.
2. Geopolitical Conflict: A worldwide conflict between two different political ideologies.
3. Limited War: As opposed to unlimited war, combatants intentionally limit the extent and scope of warfare.
4. Vietnamization: An attempt by the Americans to leave the conduct of the War to South Vietnam.
5. Winston Churchill: British prime minister during World War II.

Option 2 – Essay:

America and Russia wanted the same thing. This was a strange war. Other wars were fought to preserve honor—like the Franco Prussian War, or to keep the balance of power—like the Napoleonic Wars. Perhaps there was a precipitating event—like World War I. Some wars were provoked by a dastardly attack—like World War II. Some wars were mistakes—like the French and Indian War. But this war, the Cold War, was the first war fought—and it was a war no doubt about it, even though it was not fought with tanks and weapons—between two victors to preserve geopolitical fault lines to maintain a buffer between itself and its perceived enemies.

Chapter 17 Exam Options

Option 1 – Matching:

1. Thaumatrope: A card with different pictures on either side so that when the card is rapidly twirled, the images appear to combine.
2. Phenakistiscope: The phenakistoscope was an early animation device that used the persistence of vision principle to create an illusion of motion.
3. Daguerreotype: The first commercially successful photographic process.
4. Vitascope: Vitascope was an early film projector first demonstrated in 1895.
5. Tom Mix: Early cinema cowboy star.

Option 2 – Essay:

A Hollywood Idol would have a conflict with his parents on the silver screen and that conflict would be repeated in thousands of families across America. The cinema was the great culture creator—until the television.

Chapter 18 Exam Options

Option 1 – Matching:

1. Rock 'n' Roll: A type of music emerging in the 1950s.
2. Blues: The name given to both a musical form and a music genre that originated in African-American communities of primarily the "Deep South" of the United States.
3. Jazz: A musical style that originated at the beginning of the 20th century in African American communities in the Southern United States.
4. Ragtime: Ragtime is an original musical genre that enjoyed its peak popularity between 1900 and 1918.
5. Dixieland: Dixieland music, sometimes referred to as Hot jazz, Early Jazz or New Orleans jazz, is a style of jazz music which developed in New Orleans at the start of the 20th century.

Option 2 – Essay:

Answers will vary.

Chapter 19 Exam Options

Option 1 – Matching:

1. Social Revolution: Dynamic changes in family, government, and society.
2. Youth Culture: A term that describes the growing influence of youth.
3. Scientific Revolution: Dynamic changes in technological progress, including fields of medicine and media.
4. 20th Century movement: The nation's population shifted from the Northeast to the Sunbelt.
5. Concentration camps: Massive prison-holding facilities often used to slaughter large groups of people.

Option 2 – Essay:

The author believes that God is lifting up a new generation of born-again, evangelical leaders who will populate the culture-creating centers of this nation. He does not know what or when the tipping point will occur. But when it does there will be an unprecedented revival.

Chapter 20 Exam Options

Option 1 – Matching:

1. Ralph Nader: An early leader of the consumer movement.

2. Ghettoization: A term to describe the movement of African-Americans into poor sections of the city.
3. Black Nationalism: African-American movement that celebrated African-American exclusionism.
4. White Guilt: A term to describe guilt over racial relations.
5. Racism: A belief system based on the concept that people are divided into races, and that certain races are superior to others.

Option 2 – Essay:

Answers will vary.

Chapter 21 Exam Options

Option 1 – Matching:

1. Executive Branch: Composed of the president and his cabinet.
2. Legislative Branch: Congress and its influence.
3. Judicial Branch: The court system.
4. Federal government of the United States: Composed of the executive branch, the legislative branch, and the judicial branch.
5. Government: Refers to the way people arbitrate, control, and live their lives.

Option 2 – Essay:

The court ruled 6–3 that acceptance by students of federal educational grants did fall under the regulatory requirements of Title IX, but limited the application to the school's financial aid department. In 1988, new legislation subjected every department of any educational institution that received federal funding to Title IX requirements. In response, Grove City College withdrew from the Stafford loan program entirely beginning with the 1988–89 academic year, and established its own loan program. So both the courts and Grove City won and lost.

Chapter 22 Exam Options

Option 1 – Matching:

1. Mercury Projects: Early NASA efforts to put a man in space.
2. Sputnik: Russian satelitte—the first one in space.
3. Gemini: NASA efforts to understand space travel.
4. Apollo: NASA efforts to go to the moon.
5. Wernher Von Braun: Former Nazi German space scientist who helped the Americans.

Option 2 – Essay:

Answers will vary.

Chapter 23 Exam Options

Option 1 – Matching:

Leave it to Beaver: A successful sitcom television show in the 1950s.

Feminism: An assertive women's rights movement.

Fatherhood: A movement to save fathers' roles in families.

Traditional family: A typical family from the 1960s that comprised a working father, a homemaker mother, and their two kids.

Galatians 3:28: Biblical passage that speaks of the equal status of all who are in Christ.

Option 2 – Essay:

Besides the fact that the majority of Americans do not live in nuclear families, the notion of a happy, wholesome American family struggling to make the right choices under God and government leadership, is naïve, even laughable aberration.

Chapter 24 Exam Options

Option 1 – Matching:

City of God, City of Satan: Terms coined to describe a notion that Satan wants to own the city.

Urbanization: A movement in history toward a majority of world dwellers living in the city.

History Maker: A term to describe someone who really changes history.

Antioch Church: A city church that welcomed diversity of all types.

Skyscraper: Tall buildings to accommodate the maximum number of people within a minimum space.

Option 2 – Essay:

Answers will vary. I would make sure we are a neighborhood church as well as a commuting church. I would preach the Gospel but also respond to the needs of the community.

Chapter 25 Exam Options

Option 1 – Matching:

Post-Modernism: Post-1990 movement that emphasizes the subjective.

2. Richard Rorty: A philosopher who emphasized the use of language.

3. Immanuel Kant: A philosopher who saw experience as the primary core reality.

4. Post-modern architecture: Created new designs and new visions in buildings.

5. Grant Wacker: Insists that the growth of the Church has, and must, employ whatever tools God provides — including the media.

Option 2 – Essay:

David Wagner, in "The Family and the Constitution," in *First Things Journal*, August/September, 1994. Wagner argues that the family is under assault from Post-Modernism. In the name of individuality" Wagner argues, the state is radically changing the notion of "family" by advancing notions of "individualism." There can be no biblical or any other norm.

Chapter 26 Exam Options

Option 1 – Matching:

1. Tea Party Movement: A conservative political movement whose main purpose is to decrease government control of American life.

2. Recession of 2008: The most serious economic downturn since the Great Depression.

3. Distinctive food: Became a defining symbol of national identity in the 19th century.

4. Free market capitalists: Assert that government intervention merely drags out recessions and depressions.

5. Edward Gibbon: Author of *The Decline and Fall of the Roman Empire*.

Option 2 – Essay:

A Christian must obey his Lord and His word even if his country, a good country, asks him to do otherwise.

Chapter 27 Exam Options

Option 1 – Matching:

1. Oswald Chambers: Early 20th century saint who wrote a very popular devotional *My Utmost for His Highest*.

2. Clive Staples (C.S.) Lewis: Professor of Medieval and Renaissance English literature at Cambridge University.

3. Thomas Merton: One of the most influential American spiritual writers of the 20th century.

4. Francis Schaeffer: Moved to Switzerland in 1948 as a missionary, and founded L'Abri (the Shelter) Fellowship with his wife, Edith.

5. Mother Teresa: Her Missionaries of Charity grew from 12 to thousands serving the "poorest of the poor" in 450 centers around the world.

Option 2 – Essay:

Carl Henry, C. S. Lewis, Billy Graham, Mother Teresa, R. C. Sproul, Sr. Answers will vary.

Chapter 28 Exam Options

Option 1 – Matching:

1. University of Bologna: The first university.

2. King Belshazzar's Feast: A metaphor based on the Book of Daniel to explain the university.

3. Harvard University Charter: A charter stating the mission and purpose of Harvard University.

4. University: An institution of advanced education and research that grants academic degrees.

5. Christo et Ecclesiae: Harvard's motto for 300 years, which meant "for Christ and church."

Option 2 – Essay:

Answers will vary.

Chapter 29 Exam Options

Option 1 – Matching:

1. Iranian Hostages: The Iran hostage crisis was a diplomatic crisis between Iran and the United States where 52 Americans were held hostage for 444 days from November 4, 1979 to January 20, 1981.

2. Oil Crisis: Shortages of oil that caused spiked oil prices.

3. Robert Stobaugh: Author of *Future Energy*.

4. Assassination: Murder of a political official.

5. T. S. Eliot: Perhaps the best poet and dramatist of the 20th century.

Option 2 – Essay:

Answers will vary.

Chapter 30 Exam Options

Option 1 – Matching:

1. European Union: The union of continental Europe after the Iron Curtain fell in 1990.

2. European Parliament: The governing body of the European Union.

3. Jeremy Rifkin: A controversial New Left historian.

4. United States of Europe: A term used by Victor Hugo during a speech at the International Peace Congress in 1849.

5. Common Market: Advances free trade and uniform standards.

Option 2 – Essay:

Until and if the European Union has a joint military, perhaps it will never be a political threat. The EU will pose another perhaps more important challenge, that is a long-term threat to American economic predominance. If the Euro replaces the dollar as the preferred currency we could be in trouble. Mark S. Watson, writes, "If American policy makers can allow another big player on the scene, America could find itself with a strengthened ally. If however less rational and reactionary elements should get a hold of the foreign policy apparatus, then a period of tension and perhaps even a degree of animosity could ensue, though not for long." http://www.markswatson.com/eu_1.htm

Chapter 31 Exam Options

Option 1 – Matching:

1. Manchus: Late 19th-century ruling Chinese family.

2. Tiananmen Square: Historical gathering place of radicals and revolutionaries.

3. Chiang Kaishek: Nationalist leader of China.

4. Mao Zedong: Communist leader of Chinia.

5. Great Leap Forward: Economic and social revolution in the 1960s.

Option 2 – Essay:

No, we should encourage democracy and we should refuse to do business with any country that has a reputation of poor human rights. China can be Communist and we can do business, but we should insist on changes in certain policies—such as one-child policies that inevitably lead to infanticide and abortion of female children.

Chapter 32 Exam Options

Option 1 – Matching:

1. Terrorism: Systematic violence against a government on behalf of a cause.

2. Collateral Damage: Injury to non-combatant civilians.

3. Jewish Zealots: Radical Jewish Zionists who sought freedom for Israel.

- Religious extremists: Often view modernization efforts as corrupting influences on traditional culture.
- Sons of Liberty: Organized into patriotic Chapters as a result of the Stamp Tax of 1765.

Option 2 – Essay:

The taking of innocent lives for a cause, however laudable, is never an acceptable tactic.

Chapter 33 Exam Options

Option 1 – Matching:

1. Pandemic: A worldwide disease epidemic.
2. Global Warming: A theory that the world is warming.
3. Eschatology: Study of the end times.
4. Parousia: The Second Coming of Jesus Christ.
5. Premillennialism: A belief of the end times held by a large percentage of Christians during the first three centuries of the Christian era.

Option 2 – Essay:

God is in absolute control. He has determined our future so we have nothing to fear.

Chapter 34 Exam Options

Option 1 – Matching:

1. Futurology: The prediction of the future.
2. Globalized World: A world who draws its vision and resources from the entire globe.
3. Fortress Nation: A concept of a world that is paraochial and self-serving.
4. Orson Welles: Gave a live performance of H.G. Wells' science fiction novel *The War of the Worlds*.
5. Hindenburg: The German passenger zeppelin airship that caught fire and was destroyed in 1937.

Option 2 – Essay:

Yes! But I believe that you, young people, led by the Holy Spirit, can turn this world around!

Equipping students to Live, Write, & Speak

Communication Courses from a Biblical Worldview

Each 34-week course develops written & verbal communication skills

Chapters include one daily lesson Monday through Thursday with concept builders, weekly writing assignment/speech, and chapter exam on Friday.

Learning activities include writing, essays, research paper, & public speaking

Skills for Rhetoric helps Jr. high students develop the skills necessary to communicate powerfully through writing and to articulate their thoughts clearly. Dr. Stobaugh weaves biblical concepts, readings, and applications throughout the curriculum to help equip students to stand firm in their faith.

nlpg.com/rhetoric

Skills for Literary Analysis equips Jr. high students to analyze classic literary genres, discern authors' worldviews, and apply biblical standards. Dr. Stobaugh's instruction helps to empower students to be more effective Christian apologists.

nlpg.com/literaryanalysis

Skills for Rhetoric (student)
Paper (300 pages)
Price: $34.99
ISBN: 978-0-89051-710-9

Teacher:
Paper (294 pages)
Price: $15.99
ISBN: 978-0-89051-711-6

Skills for Literary Analysis (student)
Paper (382 pages)
Price: $34.99
ISBN: 978-0-89051-712-3

Teacher:
Paper (294 pages)
Price: $15.99
ISBN: 978-0-89051-713-0

Master Books®
A Division of New Leaf Publishing Group
www.masterbooks.net

Place your order at masterbooks.net or call 800-999-3777

Parent Lesson Plan — Promotion

Now turn your favorite **Master Books** into curriculum! Each Parent Lesson Plan (PLP) includes:

- An easy-to-follow, one-year educational calendar
- Helpful worksheets, quizzes, tests, and answer keys
- Additional teaching helps and insights
- Complete with all you need to quickly and easily begin your education program today!

ELEMENTARY ZOOLOGY

1 year
4th – 6th

Package Includes: *World of Animals, Dinosaur Activity Book, The Complete Aquarium Adventure, The Complete Zoo Adventure, Parent Lesson Planner*

5 Book Package
978-0-89051-747-5 $84.99

SCIENCE STARTERS: ELEMENTARY PHYSICAL & EARTH SCIENCE

1 year
3rd – 6th grade

6 Book Package Includes: *Forces & Motion –Student, Student Journal, and Teacher; The Earth – Student, Teacher & Student Journal; Parent Lesson Planner*

6 Book Package
978-0-89051-748-2 $51.99

SCIENCE STARTERS: ELEMENTARY CHEMISTRY & PHYSICS

1 year
3rd – 6th grade

Package Includes: *Matter – Student, Student Journal, and Teacher; Energy – Student, Teacher, & Student Journal; Parent Lesson Planner*

7 Book Package
978-0-89051-749-9 $54.99

INTRO TO METEOROLOGY & ASTRONOMY

1 year
7th – 9th grade
½ Credit

Package Includes: *The Weather Book; The Astronomy Book; Parent Lesson Planner*

3 Book Package
978-0-89051-753-6 $44.99

INTRO TO OCEANOGRAPHY & ECOLOGY

1 year
7th – 9th grade
½ Credit

Package Includes: *The Ocean Book; The Ecology Book; Parent Lesson Planner*

3 Book Package
978-0-89051-754-3 $45.99

INTRO TO SPELEOLOGY & PALEONTOLOGY

1 year
7th – 9th grade
½ Credit

Package Includes: *The Cave Book; The Fossil Book; Parent Lesson Planner*

3 Book Package
978-0-89051-752-9 $44.9

CONCEPTS OF MEDICINE & BIOLOGY

1 year
7th – 9th grade
½ Credit

Package Includes: *Exploring the History of Medicine; Exploring the World of Biology; Parent Lesson Planner*

3 Book Package
978-0-89051-756-7 $40.9

CONCEPTS OF MATHEMATICS & PHYSICS

1 year
7th – 9th grade
½ Credit

Package Includes: *Exploring the World of Mathematics; Exploring the World of Physics; Parent Lesson Planner*

3 Book Package
978-0-89051-757-4 $40.9

CONCEPTS OF EARTH SCIENCE & CHEMISTRY

1 year
7th – 9th grade
½ Credit

Package Includes: *Exploring Planet Earth; Exploring the World of Chemistry; Parent Lesson Planner*

3 Book Package
978-0-89051-755-0 $40.9

THE SCIENCE OF LIFE: BIOLOGY

1 year
8th – 9th grade
½ Credit

Package Includes: *Building Blocks in Science; Building Blocks in Life Science; Parent Lesson Planner*

3 Book Package
978-0-89051-758-1 $44.9

BASIC PRE-MED

1 year
8th – 9th grade
½ Credit

Package Includes: *The Genesis of Germs; The Building Blocks in Life Science; Parent Lesson Planner*

3 Book Package
978-0-89051-759-8 $43.9

INTRO TO ASTRONOMY

1 year
7th – 9th grade
½ Credit

Package Includes: *The Stargazer's Guide to the Night Sky; Parent Lesson Planner*

2 Book Package
978-0-89051-760-4 $47.99

INTRO TO ARCHAEOLOGY & GEOLOGY

1 year
7th – 9th
½ Credit

Package Includes: *The Archaeology Book; The Geology Book; Parent Lesson Planner*

3 Book Package
978-0-89051-751-2 $45.99

SURVEY OF SCIENCE HISTORY & CONCEPTS

1 year
10th – 12th grade
1 Credit

Package Includes: *The World of Mathematics; The World of Physics; The World of Biology; The World of Chemistry; Parent Lesson Planner*

5 Book Package
978-0-89051-764-2 $72.99

SURVEY OF SCIENCE SPECIALTIES

1 year
10th – 12th grade
1 Credit

Package Includes: *The Cave Book; The Fossil Book; The Geology Book; The Archaeology Book; Parent Lesson Planner*

5 Book Package
978-0-89051-765-9 $81.99

SURVEY OF ASTRONOMY

1 year
10th – 12th grade
1 Credit

Package Includes: *The Stargazers Guide to the Night Sky; Our Created Moon; Taking Back Astronomy; Our Created Moon DVD; Created Cosmos DVD; Parent Lesson Planner*

4 Book, 2 DVD Package
978-0-89051-766-6 $113.99

GEOLOGY & BIBLICAL HISTORY

1 year
8th – 9th
1 Credit

Package Includes: *Explore the Grand Canyon; Explore Yellowstone; Explore Yosemite & Zion National Parks; Your Guide to the Grand Canyon; Your Guide to Yellowstone; Your Guide to Zion & Bryce Canyon National Parks; Parent Lesson Planner.*

4 Book, 3 DVD Package
978-0-89051-750-5 $108.99

PALEONTOLOGY: LIVING FOSSILS

1 year
10th – 12th grade
½ Credit

Package Includes: *Living Fossils, Living Fossils Teacher Guide, Living Fossils DVD; Parent Lesson Planner*

3 Book, 1 DVD Package
978-0-89051-763-5 $66.99

LIFE SCIENCE ORIGINS & SCIENTIFIC THEORY

1 year
10th – 12th grade
1 Credit

Package Includes: *Evolution: the Grand Experiment, Teacher Guide, DVD; Living Fossils, Teacher Guide, DVD; Parent Lesson Planner*

5 Book, 2 DVD Package
978-0-89051-761-1 $144.99

NATURAL SCIENCE THE STORY OF ORIGINS

1 year
10th – 12th grade
½ Credit

Package Includes: *Evolution: the Grand Experiment; Evolution: the Grand Experiment Teacher's Guide; Evolution: the Grand Experiment DVD; Parent Lesson Planner*

3 Book, 1 DVD Package
978-0-89051-762-8 $71.99

ADVANCED PRE-MED STUDIES

1 year
10th – 12th grade
1 Credit

Package Includes: *Building Blocks in Life Science; The Genesis of Germs; Body by Design; Exploring the History of Medicine; Parent Lesson Planner*

5 Book Package
978-0-89051-767-3 $76.99

BIBLICAL ARCHAEOLOGY

1 year
10th – 12th grade
1 Credit

Package Includes: *Unwrapping the Pharaohs; Unveiling the Kings of Israel; The Archaeology Book; Parent Lesson Planner.*

4 Book Package
978-0-89051-768-0 $99.99

CHRISTIAN HERITAGE

1 year
10th – 12th grade
1 Credit

Package Includes: *For You They Signed; Lesson Parent Planner*

2 Book Package
978-0-89051-769-7 $50.99

SCIENCE STARTERS: ELEMENTARY GENERAL SCIENCE & ASTRONOMY

1 year
3rd – 6th grade

Package Includes: *Water & Weather – Student, Student Journal, and Teacher; The Universe – Student, Teacher, & Student Journal; Parent Lesson Planner*

7 Book Package
978-0-89051-816-8 $54.99

APPLIED SCIENCE: STUDIES OF GOD'S DESIGN IN NATURE

1 year
7th – 9th grade
1 Credit

Package Includes: *Made in Heaven, Champions of Invention, Discovery of Design, & Parent Lesson Planner*

4 Book Package
978-0-89051-812-0 $50.99

ELEMENTARY WORLD HISTORY

1 year
3rd – 6th

Package Includes: *The Big Book of History; Noah's Ark: Thinking Outside the Box (book and DVD); & Parent Lesson Planner*

3 Book, 1 DVD Package
978-0-89051-815-1 $66.96

CONCEPTS OF BIOGEOLOGY & ASTRONOMY

1 year
7th – 9th grade
½ Credit

Package Includes: *Exploring the World Around You, Exploring the World of Astronomy, & Parent Lesson Planner*

3 Book Package
978-0-89051-813-7 $41.99

ELEMENTARY GEOGRAPHY AND CULTURES

1 year
3rd – 6th grade

Package Includes: *Children's Atlas of God's World, Passport to the World, & Parent Lesson Planner*

3 Book Package
978-0-89051-814-4 $49.99

INTRO TO BIBLICAL GREEK

½ year language studies
10th – 12th
½ Credit

Package Includes: *It's Not Greek to Me DVD & Parent Lesson Planner*

1 Book, 1 DVD Package
978-0-89051-818-2 $33.99

INTRO TO ECONOMICS: MONEY, HISTORY, & FISCAL FAITH

½ year economics
10th – 12th
½ Credit

Package Includes: *Bankruptcy of Our Nation, Money Wise DVD, & Parent Lesson Planner*

2 Book, 4 DVD Package
978-0-89051-811-3 $57.99

Master Books®

P.O. Box 726
Green Forest, AR 72638

Visit masterbooks.net for additional information look insides, video trailers, and more